A Study Guide Based on the Award-Winni

MW01178252

Learning From the Master

Living a Surrendered Life

Laura J. Davis

LEARNING FROM THE MASTER

ISBN: 978-1-77069-512-2

Word Alive Press
131 Cordite Road, Winnipeg, MB R3W 1S1
www.wordalivepress.ca

WORD ALIVE PRESS
Just Write!

Library and Archives Canada Cataloguing in Publication

Davis, Laura J., 1958-
Learning from the master : living a surrendered life / Laura J. Davis.

Based on the author's Come to me.
ISBN 978-1-77069-512-2

1. Jesus Christ. 2. Jesus Christ--Family. I. Title.

BT301.3.D37 2012 232.9'01 C2012-901239-4

Contents

This book is dedicated to Anne B. Davis, my mother in-law, who knew what it meant to live a life surrendered to God. Mom, you are missed every day.

Acknowledgements

I had so much fun writing this study guide for my novel *Come to Me*. Digging deeper into scripture has always been something I enjoy, as each new discovery brings me closer to the Saviour. I want to thank my editor Stephanie Nickel. Not only did she correct my typos and grammar, she was a great sounding board for a few of the theological issues I touched on in the study. Stephanie, you are a great friend and I can't thank you enough for all your help.

I would also like to thank Jen Jandavs-Hedlin of Word Alive Press. You are very patient with me. Thank you for all you do.

Of course, there would be no book at all without the loving support of my husband Jim. Honey, what would I do without you?

Finally, to my Lord and Saviour, thank you for letting me sit at Your feet and teaching me the value of surrender.

Getting Started

Would you say your life is totally "sold-out" for God? Are you completely and utterly surrendered to him? Some of you might pump your fists in the air and shout, "Yes! Hallelujah! I am a servant of God. Jesus can ask me to do anything or go anywhere, and I will do it." Like Abraham, you forge ahead into the unknown – no questions asked. Others of you might hang your heads in shame, knowing your lifestyle and attitude could use a few adjustments in that department. You want to be surrendered to God, but it's too much of a risk. You're afraid of what He might ask you to do. Like Moses, you put up a fight when you know God is calling you to do something for Him.

Like Abraham and Moses, both types of Christians eventually crumble under the weight of fear and pride. You can read their stories in the books of Genesis and Exodus. Abraham started his journey well and faced many tests along the way, the harshest, being asked to sacrifice his son Isaac. Unfortunately, when he travelled into Gerar, he became afraid the king of that land would kill him in order to take his wife. So he lied to protect himself and told everyone Sarah was his sister (Genesis 20). Moses, on the other hand, just made excuse after excuse until God got mad at him for not trusting Him with his life (Exodus 3-4).

We might think we are totally surrendered to God, but in many ways we are not. In the pages ahead, we will look at the lives of Christ, his mother, family, and disciples to learn not only what faith is about, but also what it means to be totally "sold-out" to God.

How to Get the Most out of this Workbook

Learning from the Master is designed to be used in conjunction with the novel *Come to Me*. It is suitable for a Bible study group or a book club. Ideally, you will read the relevant chapters in *Come to Me* and then go through the corresponding session in the workbook, using your Bible as well. The point of using the novel is to give you a glimpse into the life of Christ through His relationships with family and His disciples and to see a life totally surrendered to God. However, if you can't afford the novel, you can still get a lot out of using only the workbook and the Scriptures.

The most effective way to use this workbook is to go through it on your own. This allows you ample time to digest what you've read and apply it to your life, even if you are going to discuss the questions in a group afterward. Some of the questions are personal; others will provoke discussion. So the best way to use the book is to go through it on your own first and then come together each week to discuss what you've learned.

How to Use the Book in a Group

If you are trying to squeeze all forty-one chapters of Come to Me, into a twelve-week course for your Bible study group, it can be done. It is always best to appoint a facilitator for your group. A facilitator is not a teacher, but rather someone who keeps the discussion on track and on time. Not every question needs to be answered. Some may prove more time consuming than others. It is up to the facilitator to decide when to move on.

Each session begins with Chit-Chat. Take this time to relax and get to know one another, using the questions provided. These questions are geared to highlight the lesson, but feel free to ask your own. Plan your time accordingly. If your class is only one hour, do not take more than ten minutes with these questions.

After Chit-Chat, begin your session with an opening prayer, inviting the Holy Spirit to lead and guide you as you look into God's Holy Word.

Finish each session with enough time for prayer.

Note: *Come to Me* has remained faithful to the Protestant Scriptures and therefore, does not include Catholic doctrine, except for two occurrences where I elected to keep names that come from Catholic tradition, that of Peter's wife (Perpetua) and the names of the Magi. I did this for two simple reasons: I liked the name Perpetua, and the names of the Magi are in so many Christmas stories that, rather than add confusion, I left them as is. I also did not keep to the Catholic belief that Mary's mother's name was Anne. I did this because of the history behind that belief and the cult that sprang from it. Hence, the name of Mary's mother is Rebekah in *Come to Me.*

Of course the issue of Mary's perpetual virginity will likely come up, as well as the belief that she did not die. Be sensitive to those who chafe against Protestant beliefs. Let them voice their concerns, but always point them back to the Scriptures.

How to Do this Study on Your Own

Read the suggested chapters in *Come to Me* if you have the book, and then go through the workbook. Don't rush. Take time to ponder what you are learning and apply it to your life. Some of my readers have chosen to use *Come to Me* during Advent and Lent. While this would take longer, it is certainly an option. I recommend using the novel and workbook any time of the year, as learning about Jesus' life and the lessons He has for us can be applied all year long.

About the Novel *Come to Me*

Step back in time and experience the life of Christ through the eyes of His mother. *Come to Me* offers the reader an intimate glimpse into the lives of Jesus and His family in a way that brings them to life. The themes of trusting in God and surrendering to Him are evident throughout this remarkable story.

From the cradle to the cross, *Come to Me* speaks to the hearts of those who are seeking, and deepens the faith of long-time believers. It is a moving tale of the life of Christ from the mother who raised Him to become the Saviour of the world.

"Author Laura Davis examines the life of Mary, mother of Jesus. We hear the tender maternal love, the worry, the fears and the awe-inspiring faith that allowed her to become the vessel to carry God's only Son. Laura writes with a gentle hand and yet doesn't hold back on the reality of the cross. It is a fascinating perspective and a wonderful read."

~Donna Dawson
Author of the award-winning novel *Vengeance*
Creative Writing Instructor, Fanshawe College

Come to Me is available through Amazon, Chapters/Indigo, GreatCanadianAuthors.com and wherever fine Christian books are sold.

Faith and Family

— Read Chapters 1 and 2 of *Come to Me* —

If you grew up in a Christian home, you probably said grace at your meals, attended church every Sunday, and had regular prayer and Bible study times. If you were like me, however, you only said grace when grandparents came to visit. Growing up, prayer times consisted of "Now I lay me down to sleep..." We learned The Lord's Prayer in school. All of these things are good, but reciting prayers by rote and getting perfect attendance in Sunday school does not a Christian make. Faith in God and exercising that faith are essential to your Christian walk. So, how do we *learn* faith? Is it acquired through osmosis just by being part of a Christian family? Is it something that grows over time? How can we grow in faith? More importantly, how do we instill our faith in God in our children and other family members?

In the selected chapters for today, we get a brief glimpse of what married life was like for Mary. We consider her concerns as she thinks about her marriage to Joseph. We see a willing worker and faithful servant of God.

It is eleven years after Jesus' death and resurrection. *Come to Me* opens with Mary lost in thought as she waits for the apostle Luke to arrive. As you read these chapters, remember Mary lived in a small community of about 400 people. She probably knew everyone in her village. In fact, most extended families lived close to one another. As she reflects on her life, keep this in mind.

Faith

Chit-Chat: When you were growing up, who taught you about God? How important was God in your family?

“[4]Hear, O Israel: The Lord our God, the Lord is one. [5]Love the Lord your God with all your heart and with all your soul and with all your strength” (Deuteronomy 6:4-5).

This is called the Shema. It is a term given to a set of daily prayers recited by members of the Jewish faith. The Shema is recited twice a day, during morning and evening prayers and is the last thing on the lips of the dying. It is considered a commandment, or mitzvah, separate from the commandment simply to pray. Joseph had carved this prayer into Mary’s bench. What do these verses mean to you?

Take a moment to examine yourself. Do you remember what it felt like when you first fell in love? I do. My relationship with my husband was a long distance one, and we ran up some very expensive phone bills talking to each other every day. I couldn’t stand being away from him. He was always on my mind. My heart soared when the phone rang, and when I saw him in person, I was over the moon. I loved my husband with all my heart, soul, and mind. My question to you is this: Do you love God that way?

As the stepson of a devout Jew, Jesus would have been under Joseph’s instruction and that of the local leaders of his synagogue. The Shema would have been one of the first prayers Joseph taught Jesus. As we read further in the verse, we can see why Jesus knew the Scriptures so well. Moses had just given the Israelites the Ten Commandments.

“[4] Hear, O Israel: The Lord our God, the Lord is one. [5] Love the Lord your God with all your heart and with all your soul and with all your strength. [6] These commandments that I give you today are to be upon your hearts. [7] Impress them on your children. Talk about them when you sit at home and when you walk along the road, when you lie down and when you get up. [8] Tie them as symbols on your hands and bind them on your foreheads. [9] Write them on the doorframes of your houses and on your gates” (Deuteronomy 6:4-9).

In addition to loving the Lord with all our heart, soul, and mind, what does verse six command?

What does verse seven command parents to do?

Verse eight commands, "Tie them as symbols on your hands and bind them on your foreheads." Today you will see Orthodox Jews doing just that. Some wear little boxes on their heads called tefillin. They also wear leather straps on their arms in obedience to this command, all to remind them to love the Lord and obey Him. This is the background Jesus came from. His life was steeped in tradition and the Torah (Old Testament). His parents, who were chosen by God, would have taught him well.

Look at verse seven again. How was Jesus' life an example of the Shema?

Family

As Mary waited for Luke, she recalled her conversation with her nephew John. You might be surprised to discover that James and John, the "Sons of Thunder" as Jesus called them, were actually His cousins. The next few scriptures will help you discover this for yourself.

"21 Going on from there, he saw two other brothers, James son of Zebedee and his brother John. They were in a boat with their father Zebedee, preparing their nets. Jesus called them, 22 and immediately they left the boat and their father and followed him" (Matthew 4:21-22).

"These are the names of the twelve apostles: first, Simon (who is called Peter) and his brother Andrew; James son of Zebedee, and his brother John" (Matthew 10:2).

What were the names of Zebedee's sons?

"55 Many women were there, watching from a distance. They had followed Jesus from Galilee to care for his needs. 56 Among them were Mary Magdalene, Mary the mother of James and Joses, and the mother of Zebedee's sons" (Matthew 27:55-56).

Who was present at the cross?

"40 Some women were watching from a distance. Among them were Mary Magdalene, Mary the mother of James the younger and of Joses, and Salome" (Mark 15:40).

Look at the previous verse again and then read the one above. What was the name of Zebedee's wife?

Who were Jesus' cousins?

As discussed earlier, Nazareth was a very small village and extended family members tended to live close to each other. While this wasn't always the case – Mary's cousin Elizabeth lived more than 100 kilometers away from her – it was the norm. Already we see the close family ties Jesus grew up with and how the strong ties of faith in God kept them together.

"1 And God spoke all these words: 2 'I am the Lord your God, who brought you out of Egypt, out of the land of slavery. 3 You shall have no other gods before me. 4 You shall not make for yourself an idol in the form of anything in heaven above or on the earth beneath or in the waters below. 5 You shall not bow down to them or worship them; for I, the Lord your God, am a jealous God, punishing the children for the sin of the fathers to the third and fourth generation of those who hate me, 6 but showing love to a thousand generations of those who love me and keep my commandments'" (Exodus 20:1-6).

In the novel, Luke is worried that his respect for Mary would turn into adoration or worship. The early converts in Antioch, particularly the women, had this problem, as the book suggests. But what does God say about idol worship?

What do we learn about God from the verses above?

Put yourself in Mary's shoes. She is a servant of God and a Jew, brought up to honour God and place Him first. How do you think she would react to people worshipping her?

Is the veneration of Mary scriptural or in any way appropriate for Christians?

Tradition tells us Mary was a young girl of no more than fourteen or fifteen. Some scholars suggest she may have been as young as twelve. Her betrothal to Joseph was not how we view engagements today. It was a binding contract. Most betrothals lasted for a year or more. During this time, Mary was considered by all to be Joseph's wife, even though she still lived at home with her parents and they had not yet consummated their marriage.

Mary is like any young teenager thinking about her wedding day. Contrast this with the promiscuous lifestyle of today's teens. What is the missing element in teenage lives today that has led to such immoral behaviour?

What or who are the major influencers of this behaviour?

Having a better idea now of how Jesus was raised, we know how important a role parents have in instructing their children spiritually. Teaching them to believe in God and to obey Him is one thing. Being an example of faith to them is another. What can you do this week to show your children, family, or friends that you love the Lord with all your heart, soul, and mind?

Prayer: Lord, faith and family go hand in hand. Help us give You first place in our lives. Help us be an example to our children and a witness to our neighbours as we live out our faith. Keep us from putting anything else above you. May You find us faithful when You come again. In Jesus' name. Amen.

Trusting God

—— Read Chapters 3 and 4 of *Come to Me* ——

Have you ever stopped to think about how God chose Mary to be His vessel for Christ's entrance into the world? We know from the Scriptures that God knows each one of us intimately, before we are even born. Take a moment to read the verses below and contemplate how much God loves you and how much attention to detail He has put into your life.

"13 For you created my inmost being; you knit me together in my mother's womb. 14 I praise you because I am fearfully and wonderfully made; your works are wonderful, I know that full well. 15 My frame was not hidden from you when I was made in the secret place. When I was woven together in the depths of the earth, 16 your eyes saw my unformed body. All the days ordained for me were written in your book before one of them came to be" (Psalm 139:13-16).

"Before I formed you in the womb I knew you, before you were born I set you apart; I appointed you as a prophet to the nations" (Jeremiah 1:5).

Do you marvel at the wonders of God? Even before you were born, He appointed a set number of days for you to live. According to Ephesians 2:10, you were "created in Christ Jesus to do good works, which God prepared in advance for us to do." Jeremiah 29:11 is my favourite verse. It says, "'For I know the plans I have for you,' declares the Lord. 'Plans to prosper you and not to harm you. Plans to give you hope and a future.'"

God's plans and His ways are not, unfortunately, something we always adhere to. The scripture is true when it says, "We all like sheep have gone astray" (Isaiah 53:6). We have the unbelievable God-given ability of freewill, the right to choose to obey God or disobey Him. Amazingly, He knows what we will say before we say it and what we will do before we do it. Yet even when we disobey and do that which we know will displease Him, He does not give up on us. Instead, He continues to love us. So much so, He decided to send His Son to earth to teach us how to live. And He chose a young maiden whose days He had ordained before she was born. He knew her heart, and He knew she was obedient to Him. Mary was the perfect vessel to bring the Son of God into the world.

Today I want to look at the reactions of Mary and Zechariah toward the angel Gabriel. Each of these servants of God was prepared in advance for God's good works. He had ordained their days and knew what they would do. Yet their reactions were different. As you go through the lesson today, I want you to think about the fact that God has a plan for you too. It is a plan for your good. The question you need to ask yourself is this: How much do I trust Him with my life?

Chit-Chat: Is it easy for you to trust God? Why or why not?

Read Luke 1:26-38.

Twice the angel Gabriel tells Mary she is highly favoured. The Greek term in verse 28 is translated "charitoō" (khä-rē-to'-ō) and means three different things that all apply to Mary:

- to make graceful – charming, lovely, agreeable
- to peruse with grace, compass with favour
- to honour with blessings

In verse 30, Gabriel tells Mary that she has found favour with God, and it means something slightly different. The root "charis" (khä'-rēs) in this case means:

- grace
- that which affords joy, pleasure, delight, sweetness, charm, loveliness; grace of speech

What character qualities did God bestow upon Mary?

How did God look upon Mary? And how did He view what He was asking of her?

Can you imagine being so loved and respected by God that He would honour you in such a way? What is your biggest fear when saying yes to God?

Mary obediently surrendered to God's desires for her life. God was pleased to honour her by using her for His good purposes. Mary knew she was about to face a world full of trouble and hurt when her friends and family discovered her pregnant. Yet she said yes to God.

When faced with the impossible or even the unknown, how do you react? Whom do you run to first – friends, family, or God?

What we consider troubles and trials, God may consider blessings. How then should we react to bad news?

Has God ever asked you to do something you found too difficult? How did you respond? What did you learn?

God looked on Mary with favour because she was surrendered to His will. How do you think God looks on you?

Read Luke 1:5-25.

What was Zechariah's job?

What was he doing when the angel Gabriel appeared?

Note: The angel Gabriel stood to the right side of the Altar of Incense. The Altar of Incense stood before the veil or the Holy of Holies, which was before the Ark of the Covenant. The Altar of Incense was gold, and the priest would burn incense on it morning and night. The incense represented the prayers of the people. Also, once a year, on the horns of the Altar of Incense, atonement was made for the people with the blood of the sin offering.

Who was our sin offering?

With this in mind, consider where Gabriel stood. Does God leave anything to chance?

Did Gabriel have good news for Zechariah? How did Zechariah react to it?

Compare Zechariah's reaction to the news from Gabriel with Mary's. How did they differ?

Do you ever doubt God? Why or why not?

Examine yourself now and be honest. Have you believed in Jesus as your Saviour yet failed to trust Him fully with your life? Why?

From Mary and Zechariah, we know God can use us no matter what our response. We also know not trusting Him has consequences (as Zechariah found out).Think about those times in your life when you trusted God. What happened? Was the outcome good or bad?

Now think about those times you didn't heed God's voice. What was the result?

What can you do today to have a faith as trusting as Mary's?

Prayer: Lord, it has been a long time since You sent Your heavenly angels to speak to your servants. Today we rely on Your Holy Spirit and Your Holy Word to speak to us. We admit that sometimes it is not easy to hear Your voice when so many worldly concerns are crowding You out. May we be attuned only to Your voice and obediently follow when You call. Lord, we acknowledge that trust is never easy for us. We often try to fix things on our own or run to our best friends for help. Lord, by our disobedience, we hold back the blessings You desire to pour out. Forgive us. In Jesus' name. Amen.

When Your Faith Takes a Beating

—— Read Chapters 5 and 6 of *Come to Me* ——

In the last session, we talked about trusting God. Today we will go a little further and look at what happens when doubt creeps in and our faith begins to crumble.

When I was very young in my faith and knew little of how God works, I learned this verse: "Be self-controlled and alert. Your enemy the devil prowls around like a roaring lion looking for someone to devour" (1 Peter 5:8). Unfortunately, while it made me aware of obvious sins like lying or stealing, I was never prepared for the subtle sins, those that crept in so unexpectedly I wondered how I had been sucked in so easily.

For example, in regards to tithing, I always believed God loves a cheerful giver. Because my husband Jim and I decided early in our marriage that I would be a stay-at-home mom and he would work, we knew we had to put our tithing first or we would be tempted to hold it back to make ends meet. While we always struggled to keep food on the table, we still seemed to get by—just. But we still believed it was important to tithe each week, and so we continued to do so.

One day a well-meaning soul from church suggested we wouldn't be struggling if we obeyed the Scriptures in regards to tithing. I was shocked. What did she mean? Of course we obeyed the Scriptures in that regard. That is when she introduced me to this scripture from Malachi 3:10: "'Bring the whole tithe into the storehouse, that there may be food in my house. Test me in this,' says the LORD Almighty, 'and see if I will not throw open the floodgates of heaven and pour out so much blessing that you will not have room enough for it.'"

She pointed out to me that God wanted me to test Him in regards to our tithing. She said we should give over and above our regular tithe. "The more you give," she said, "the more you will get back."

Well, we were struggling quite a bit during that time, and wondering if she was right, I decided to put God to the test, forgetting the admonition in Luke 4:12: "Do not put the Lord your God to the test."

Needless to say, the day came when we had given our very last penny to the church and I wondered when the riches were going to start flowing in. They never did. However, God did provide food for us by prodding His servants to bring us enough groceries until my husband's next paycheck. God loved us and met our needs. Yet, at the time, I was in shock that we weren't rolling in dough. We gave so much money.

Where was our return? It didn't help that my friend would shake her head in confusion and say, "You must be doing something wrong. You should be rich by now."

Oh, the subtle dangers of the prosperity gospel! Be wary of preachers who teach that God "wants the best for you, and that means a better job, new car, fancy home, more money, etc." These teachers are like wolves in sheep's clothing and think only of earthly riches, not heavenly ones.

My faith went into a tailspin. I questioned God's love for us. I questioned my faith; maybe it wasn't strong enough. I doubted the Scriptures. I stopped tithing altogether. Satan, that roaring lion, was having a field day with me. Then God spoke, and His Holy Spirit gently reminded me I was to pursue Him, not riches. What I was doing was sinful, and I needed to stop and go back to what I had done before. I felt thoroughly chastised. Yet my friend continued to prosper, and I wondered, "Why her, Lord? Why not us? Would it hurt to give us just a wee bit more each month?" But the Lord reminded me He had a plan for me and it wasn't the same plan He had for my friend.

One day she would struggle at a sudden loss of money and be like a fish out of water. She would come to me and ask, "How do you do it? How do you get by each day with only one salary?"

And I could say with assurance, "We have faith that God will provide."

Chit-Chat: Have you ever had a crisis of faith? What happened?

Read Luke 1:39-55.

Come to Me does not include the entire Song of Mary, also known as the Magnificat. Today we will look at this song.

Mary hurries to visit her cousin Elisabeth. It has been suggested by some that Mary had a crisis of faith and that is why she went to visit her cousin. She had to prove to herself what the angel Gabriel had said was true. I don't allude to that in my book. Yet some scholars believe Elisabeth hinted Mary might have had doubts when she said, "Blessed is she who has believed that the Lord would fulfill his promises to her!" I'm inclined to believe Elisabeth was comparing Mary's faith to Zechariah's. What do you think?

In Luke 1:47, how does Mary refer to God? Was she sinless?

Mary exclaims that all generations will call her blessed (vs. 48). Why? See verse 49 for the answer.

To whom does God's mercy extend and how far?

Whom has He scattered and brought down? Whom has He lifted up?

Verse 53 says, "He has filled the hungry with good things but has sent the rich away empty." Is this true? What is Mary really talking about here?

Read Luke 1: 57-80.

In chapter four, Zechariah was struck mute by the angel Gabriel for his refusal to believe in Gabriel's announcement that Elisabeth would become pregnant in her old age. There is the possibility he also lost his hearing. Look at verse 62. What do you notice?

Why, if Zechariah could hear, would his friends and family, need to "sign" to him? While I do not broach this in my book, take a moment now to contemplate the implications of this for Zechariah, to spend nine months without hearing a sound or making one, all because he doubted God.

Have you ever doubted God? Why? What happened?

"[2] Consider it pure joy, my brothers, whenever you face trials of many kinds, [3] because you know that the testing of your faith develops perseverance. [4] Perseverance must finish its work so that you may be mature and complete, not lacking anything. [5] If any of you lacks wisdom, he should ask God, who gives generously to all without finding fault, and it will be given to him. [6] But when he asks, he must believe and not doubt, because he who doubts is like a wave of the sea, blown and tossed by the wind. [7] That man should not think he will receive anything from the Lord; [8] he is a double-minded man, unstable in all he does" (James 1:2-8).

Is it okay to ask God for clarification on a matter?

Is it okay to doubt God? Why or why not?

According to verse 6, what is required of us when we seek God's will?

According to James 1:2-4, how are we to consider the trials in our life? Why?

Zechariah had nine months without a voice, possibly without hearing; nine months to contemplate the angel Gabriel's words to him; nine months to persevere in his faith. Do you think his faith was tested?

What is the first thing Zechariah did when his ordeal was over?

Both Mary and Zechariah had heavenly encounters. One, advanced in years and a priest of the Lord, doubted what he saw and heard. He lacked faith. Mary, young and innocent, trusted Gabriel and surrendered to God immediately. When is it hardest for you to believe and trust in God?

Prayer: Lord, You have prepared the way for us to find salvation. You have allowed us to encounter troubles and trials along the way as well. Help us remember that, along with the good news of your saving grace, You are, at the same time, forging our faith through the fire of tribulation. Forgive us when we lose our way. Help us now to go out into the world and share the good news of Jesus' gift of salvation with others. May we always remember You have a plan and a way for us. In Jesus' name. Amen.

God is in Control

— Read Chapters 7, 8, 9, and 10 of *Come to Me* —

We have talked about learning to trust God and how that trust is refined through trials and tribulations. Today I would like to cover three things: surrendering control, obedience, and submission. When we ignore God in the day to day matters of our lives we are effectively saying to Him, "No, I can do this without Your input." We don't want to release full control of our lives to Him. We may hear what He wants us to do but we don't obey Him. Without obedience to God, we are ignoring His will. Without submitting to His will, we miss out on the blessings He had planned for us. These three things: surrendering control, obedience and submission must be present in the life of every believer.

While Mary had three months to come to terms with the news that she would bear the Messiah, Joseph did not have that luxury. We learn in Chapter 8 of *Come to Me* that Joseph was a righteous man who wanted to be obedient to the Law. Yet, at the same time, he wanted to spare Mary from the Law's demands: that of being stoned for adultery. He was having a hard time deciding between obeying God's laws and following his heart.

During biblical times, adultery was a serious thing. If found guilty, the woman (and man) could be put to death (Leviticus 20:10). Today we see this form of punishment still in effect in Muslim countries. However, it is usually only the woman who is punished. Although we are shocked, this is a law God gave to Moses.

This law was a drastic measure on God's part. It showed His unruly and disobedient children how much He hated sin. The practice of stoning anyone caught in adultery, therefore, was to act as a deterrent. No father wants his child to suffer, and no father wants to see his child suffer because of wrong choices. God loves His children, but like any parent trying to teach his child right from wrong, He needed to put in place consequences for disobedience. Unfortunately, the children of Israel often flouted God's laws. They disobeyed the laws He set forth because they did not respect Him. Regrettably, the teachers of the Law and the Pharisees saw it as an opportunity not only to exercise their power and authority to carry out the punishment, but to lord their own self-righteousness over the people.

Read Matthew 1:18-25.

What was Joseph's sole reason for divorcing Mary?

What did the angel say to Joseph, and what was Joseph's response?

Joseph was faithful to not only Jewish laws and customs, but he obeyed Roman law as well. What does his faithful obedience say about his character, and what can it teach us today?

Mary obediently submitted to the Father's will, accepting the fact that it might lead to her stoning. She gave control of her life over to Him, trusting Him in all things. As Christian women, we are called to be obedient to our husbands. It is sometimes easier to surrender to God than our own husbands. For some of us, the word obey strikes a nerve. So much so, many young couples have asked the word be stricken from their wedding vows. What are your thoughts? Do you find it easy or hard to be obedient to your husband?

What is Control?

Control is to have power over or rule. God's will is not considered.

- A controlling person says I can do all things by myself.
- A controlling person will not include God in their plans.
- A controlling person does not easily surrender.

What is Obedience?

Obedience is submission to authority. There is a fear of consequences involved.

- We obey our boss or we lose our job.
- We obey our teachers or we fail the grade.
- We obey our parents or we are punished.
- We obey the laws of the land or we are arrested.
- We obey God or we suffer the consequences of failing to heed His warnings.

What is Submission?

Submission is obedience based on love and respect.

- I submit to my parents out of love and respect.
- I submit to my husband "as unto the Lord" out of love and respect.
- I submit to the Lord's will because I love and respect Him.
- Jesus submitted to God and gave His life for us out of love and respect.

What Submission is Not

- Submission is not allowing myself to be abused either physically or verbally, dominated, or hurt by another.
- Submission does not allow a husband to be "lord and master" over his wife. Jesus is to be his Lord and Master. He is to submit to the Heavenly Father.

"21 Submit to one another out of reverence for Christ. 22 Wives, submit to your husbands as to the Lord. 23 For the husband is the head of the wife as Christ is the head of the church, his body, of which he is the Savior" (Ephesians 5:21-23).

"34 Women should remain silent in the churches. They are not allowed to speak, but must be in submission, as the Law says. 35 If they want to inquire about something, they should ask their own husbands at home; for it is disgraceful for a woman to speak in the church" (1 Corinthians 14:34-35).

Why are these verses and others like them so offensive to women? Why does it get our dander up?

What is the first thing we are commanded to do in Ephesians 5:21-23? Why?

Does either of these verses say the husband has authority over the wife in the sense that he is lord and master?

In Strong's concordance, the word "everything" in Greek is translated "päs." It is an adjective that means "all", "whole" or "all things." Charles Spurgeon suggests this is not to be taken literally.

> "... 'The whole world is gone after him.' Did all the world go after Christ? 'Then went all Judea, and were baptized of him in Jordan.' Was all Judea, or all Jerusalem, baptized in Jordan? 'Ye are of God, little children,' and 'the whole world lieth in the wicked one.' Does 'the whole world' there mean everybody? If so, how was it, then, that there were some who were 'of God'? The words 'world' and 'all' are used in some seven or eight senses in Scripture; and it is very rarely that 'all' means all persons, taken individually. The words are generally

used to signify that Christ has redeemed some of all sorts—some Jews, some Gentiles, some rich, some poor, and has not restricted his redemption to either Jew or Gentile."

—Charles H. Spurgeon, Particular Redemption, A Sermon, 28 Feb 1858

In the same sense, in Ephesians 5:24, "everything" should not be taken literally, as it has come to be used by some men in the Christian community. It has been used as an excuse to dominate women and force them to do things they do not want to do. The whole purpose of submission out of love and respect is that it is to be shown equally, "submitting one to another." Our husbands are to love us as Christ loves the church. Therefore, submitting to anything contrary to the will of Christ would be a sin. If a husband is abusing this scripture to control his wife, then he is not submitting to Christ out of love and respect.

How does God expect husbands to love their wives?

What is the husband's responsibility toward the wife?

Whose responsibility is greater before the Lord, the husband's or the wife's?

Is surrendering to God similar to being submissive to your spouse? What do you think?

The theme of God being in control is evident throughout chapters 7, 8, 9, and 10 of *Come to Me*. Without the edict from Augustus to travel to Bethlehem, prophecy would not have been fulfilled. Without surrender and obedience to Him from both Mary and Joseph, the story could have had a totally different outcome. Are you confident that your life is surrendered to God's will?

When we relinquish control of our lives to God, trust soon follows. If we obey God's Word and submit to His will, we can rest in the knowledge that God holds us in the palm of His hand, and that can bring a follower of Christ extreme peace. Do you have that kind of peace? If not, what do you need to do?

What will total surrender to God cost you? What will happen if you ignore Him?

Prayer: Lord, the story of Mary and Joseph shows us how they surrendered all to follow You. Help us to be obedient servants who can be used for Your glory. Help us to be faithful witnesses to those who do not know you. In Jesus' name. Amen.

Are You Boldly Proclaiming Your Faith?

— Read Chapters 11, 12, and 13 of *Come to Me* —

Trust, obedience, and submission are all necessary acts of worship a believer must exhibit in order for God to work in their lives effectively. All these acts of worship help us as we relinquish control of our lives to God's loving hands. In addition to this, one more element is important as we strive to be like Jesus: the act of declaring Him before others. Unfortunately, it is the one act most Christians fear.

Chit-Chat: Is it easy or hard for you to share your faith? What gives you courage to speak up? What keeps you from talking at all?

Read Luke 2:4-20.

After reading the chapters in *Come to Me* and the Bible passage above, what impresses you most about Joseph and Mary?

During biblical times, shepherds were despised among the general populace. They were thought of as untrustworthy, illiterate, uncouth, unclean misfits. The religious leaders held them in the same regard as they did prostitutes. They were quite literally the social outcasts of their day. This is what makes their story so amazing.

Who else did the angelic host appear to the night Jesus was born?

What did the shepherds do after the angels left them?

After they saw Jesus, what did they do?

What does this make them?

Jesus came in the lowliest of manners. His birth was proclaimed by men considered outcasts by society. He was not born into a wealthy family, although He could have been. The angels did not appear to the religious leaders, although they could have. How does this make you feel, knowing God specifically sought out those considered outcasts by society to announce His coming? Does it bring you comfort to know that the great God of heaven elected to use men of little influence to announce His coming?

What is the significance of Jesus' lowly birth? What does it tell us?

When Jesus began His ministry, to whom did He minister to the most?

Have you ever felt you were not educated enough to tell others about Jesus' plan of salvation?

How does it make you feel to know God can use you no matter your position in life?

Have you ever tried to make yourself more important than you were?

Have you ever tried to do "great things" for the Lord only to have them fail? Did you ever wonder why?

Humility is extremely important for a follower of Christ. The shepherds, knowing they would be reviled, proclaimed the good news about Jesus' birth anyway. What can we learn from them?

Read Luke 2:21-39 and Leviticus 12:1-8.

Mary was recovering from childbirth, and the shepherds were now gone. According to Leviticus 12:1-4, how many days passed before Mary and Joseph took Jesus to Jerusalem?

How old was Jesus when He was presented to the Lord?

According to Luke 2:27, Simeon was moved by the Spirit to go into the temple courts. His prayer of praise in Luke 2:29-32 was confirmation that Jesus was the Messiah. Simeon said Jesus was "a light of revelation to the Gentiles and for the glory of your people Israel." What does this verse say to you?

After Simeon blessed Jesus, he turned to Mary with what is obviously a prophecy.

"[34] Then Simeon blessed them and said to Mary, his mother: 'This child is destined to cause the falling and rising of many in Israel, and to be a sign that will be spoken against, [35] so that the thoughts of many hearts will be revealed. And a sword will pierce your own soul too'" (Luke 2:34-35).

What are the three things Simeon tells Mary?

What do you think of his last statement to Mary?

Thus far in the story, how many times has God confirmed Jesus as Messiah to the people and in what ways?

Up to this point, who were the earliest or first believers?

Does God still use people today who, according to our worldly estimations, are not qualified?

Take some time now to examine yourself. Have you put off serving God or doing something God has asked you to do because you felt you weren't qualified or capable?

If God can use lowly shepherds with no degrees, money, or positions of power, is there any reason why He can't also use you to further His kingdom?

Write about a time in your life when God asked you to do something you felt was beyond your capabilities. How did you respond? If this hasn't happened yet, ask yourself this: Am I fully surrendered to be used by God no matter what He asks?

Prayer: Lord, before Jesus was conceived, You heralded His coming through angels, shepherds, stars, seers, priests, and prophets. You sent us proof before His birth and after. When we have doubts, bring those testimonies to our minds. In Jesus' name. Amen.

Does God Still Send Us Signs?

—Read Chapters 14, 15, and 16 of *Come to Me* —

Have you ever taken a moment to think about how much advance work went into the preparation of Jesus' birth? I'm not talking about the prophecies that were given hundreds of years before his birth, but all the other events that heralded Jesus' coming.

Mary and Joseph were set aside by God to raise His Son before they were even born. The edict given by Caesar Augustus to have everyone counted forced Mary and Joseph to travel to Bethlehem, thus, fulfilling prophecy. Without God moving Caesar to take a census, the young couple would have had no reason to travel there. There was the angelic host announcing the news to the shepherds. And let us not forget the star and the Magi. This is a topic even scientists have wondered about. How big was the star? How bright? Why didn't Herod and his advisors see it?

If you have not had the opportunity, I would urge you to purchase the DVD *The Star of Bethlehem*. You will be amazed at what you discover, and you will never again doubt that the star was real. This DVD will not only show you how the stars and planets announced Jesus' arrival, but it will also show you what was in the sky the day of His death. I guarantee you will be astounded by what you find. I have copies of this DVD available to purchase on my website at www.laurajdavis.com.You can also find out more about *The Star of Bethlehem* at www.bethlehemstar.net.

Today we are going to look briefly at the star and how the God of the universe cared enough to arrange the planets to announce His coming.

Note: If you decide to purchase the DVD, and if you are doing this study in a group setting, watch it next week. The following week, come back to the workbook. You will be glad you did.

Chit-Chat: Does God still send us signs today?

Who were the Magi? Were they members of the occult? Were they magicians or astronomers? Rick Larson the creator of the DVD *The Star of Bethlehem* says this:

> “Magi were often court astronomers who were consulted by the rulers of the day for guidance in affairs of state. This was also true in much earlier times. For example, during the Babylonian captivity of the Jews, some 500 years earlier, King Nebuchadnezzar kept a stable of court magi. Nebuchadnezzar made the Jewish prophet Daniel Chief Magus of his court when Daniel was able to interpret a dream the other magi could not.”
>
> – see Daniel Chapter 2 (Larson, 2009)

Can we assume these particular Magi were descended from Daniel? We do know from the writings of Philo about a school of Magi in the east. Students from this school may have descended from the Babylonian Magi of Daniel’s day. Modern day Iraq was Babylon and it is directly east of Jerusalem.

Read Matthew 2:1-16.

Where did the Magi see the star appear?

Did Herod or the chief priests realize there was a new star in the sky before the Magi arrived?

“[9] After they had heard the king, they went on their way, and the star they had seen in the east went ahead of them until it stopped over the place where the child was. [10] When they saw the star, they were overjoyed” (Matthew 2:9-10).

Herod sent the Magi to Bethlehem. The first thing they saw was the star. What did it do that was so unusual for a star?

Most Christmas stories have the Magi visiting Jesus in the stable the night He was born. Yet, when we read Matthew 2:16, we see Herod ordered the murder of all boys two years old and younger. Taking into consideration the age limit of the children, do you think Jesus was still a baby in a stable when the Magi found him?

13 When they had gone, an angel of the Lord appeared to Joseph in a dream. "Get up," he said, "take the
child and his mother and escape to Egypt. Stay there until I tell you, for Herod is going to search for the
child to kill him."
14 So he got up, took the child and his mother during the night and left for Egypt, 15 where he
stayed until the death of Herod. And so was fulfilled what the Lord had said through the prophet: "Out
of Egypt I called my son."
16 When Herod realized that he had been outwitted by the Magi, he was furious, and he gave orders
to kill all the boys in Bethlehem and its vicinity who were two years old and under, in accordance with
the time he had learned from the Magi. 17 Then what was said through the prophet Jeremiah was fulfilled: 18 "A voice is heard in Ramah, weeping and great mourning, Rachel weeping for her children and
refusing to be comforted, because they are no more."

— Matthew 2:13-18

What did Joseph do after the angel of the Lord appeared to him in a dream?

An angel has visited Joseph twice now in his dreams, once to tell him not to be afraid to take Mary as his wife and the second time as a warning to flee Bethlehem. In each instance, what is the one defining quality in Joseph that stands out to you?

What do you think of Joseph's and Mary's obedience to the Lord?

Do you always do what God tells you to do? If not, why?

Have you ever been asked by God to do something you were afraid to do? How did you respond?

We don't hear of angels appearing to people today. On the other hand, if we do, the reports are highly suspect and border on angel worship. How do you know when God is talking to you? Share your experiences of those times when you clearly heard His voice.

Does God still speak through His angels today? Scripture tells us this: "Do not forget to entertain strangers, for by so doing some people have entertained angels without knowing it" (Hebrews 13:2). Does He still speak to us through dreams and visions, as He did to Joseph? I can testify that He does. If not for a dream in which the Lord came to me over thirty years ago, I would not be a Christian today. He has revealed things to me through my dreams at least three times in the past thirty years. I have always said the only way the Lord can get my attention is when I'm asleep – because I talk too much when I'm awake.

God also speaks to us in other ways, and it is in these ways most of us hear Him. He speaks to us through:

- His Holy Word – with guidance from His Holy Spirit who inhabits all believers
- His people – the church, the family of God, who can unite with us in prayer and in the Spirit when we are seeking direction from the Lord
- Circumstances – Many times we hear God through events that happen to us repeatedly. For example, we hear from different sources the same scripture over and over again or something happens that we know can only be from the hand of God.

Does God still send us signs today? What is He saying to you?

Prayer: Lord, we often think You have no more signs for us, that the age of miracles is over. However, we know that isn't true, for we have seen Your mighty hand at work. We live in an age where prophecy is coming true, and we marvel that You, O Lord, still concern Yourself with such disobedient children. Lord, keep us from looking for signs because we know it is a wicked generation that looks for them. Instead, help us listen for Your voice. Help us recognize evidence that You are at work. May we join you in that work as obedient children. In Jesus' name. Amen.

Are You Thwarting God's Plans?

— Read Chapters 17, 18, and 19 of *Come to Me* —

We have learned from the lives of Joseph and Mary that God can speak to us and use us in extraordinary ways. God has a plan for all His children. While the plan He has for you may not be the same one He has for me, His plans are still the best. Still, when something bad happens to us, like illness or a tragedy of some kind, we wonder if God really is near and if He is listening to us.

Mary and Joseph must have wondered the same thing when they had to escape Herod's wrath and leave Bethlehem. As the book suggests, Joseph may well have assumed Jesus was to be raised near the temple in Jerusalem. Yet God moved in their lives and warned them to flee for Jesus' safety. He warned them before Herod had even begun his persecution and sent them to a land so far away and foreign to them I bet they wondered, at times, what God was thinking.

Chit-Chat: Have you ever had the feeling that what God was asking you to do was irrational or that He had the wrong person for the job? How did you react?

13 When they had gone, an angel of the Lord appeared to Joseph in a dream. "Get up," he said, "take the child and his mother and escape to Egypt. Stay there until I tell you, for Herod is going to search for the child to kill him."

14 So he got up, took the child and his mother during the night and left for Egypt, 15 where he stayed until the death of Herod. And so was fulfilled what the Lord had said through the prophet: "Out of Egypt I called my son."

—Matthew 2:13-15

We know that Joseph, Mary, and Jesus escaped to Egypt, and archaeological evidence verifies there was a huge Jewish population in the eastern part of the city of Alexandria. Have you ever had to move to a new home or city? What about a new country? Were you scared? Excited? How do you think Joseph and Mary felt?

What were your impressions of the way Joseph and Mary's life in Egypt was depicted in *Come to Me*?

As Jesus grew older and they settled into their new life in Egypt, once again an angel came to Joseph and told him to go back to Israel. Joseph assumed God meant he was to go to Bethlehem, but when he learned Herod's son was reigning, he feared for Jesus' safety and wondered what to do. Again, the Lord answered him in a dream. He told them to go to Galilee. So they went full-circle and were in their hometown of Nazareth once again. So many moves, fears, and changes in their lives, and all of them came from the hand of God.

Joseph received instruction from the Lord at least four times through dreams. In our last lesson, we discussed how God talks to us (His Holy Word, His people, circumstances, and dreams). Have you ever had a dream where you thought the Lord was talking to you?

Come to Me examines Mary's feelings of guilt in regards to Herod's evil plans (pages 117-119). What did you think of this? How do you react when bad things happen to good people?

Do you find it hard to trust God when trials or difficulties come your way? How do you keep your faith?

41 Every year his parents went to Jerusalem for the Feast of the Passover. 42 When he was twelve years old,
they went up to the Feast, according to the custom. 43 After the Feast was over, while his parents were
returning home, the boy Jesus stayed behind in Jerusalem, but they were unaware of it. 44 Thinking he
was in their company, they traveled on for a day. Then they began looking for him among their relatives
and friends. 45 When they did not find him, they went back to Jerusalem to look for him. 46 After three
days they found him in the temple courts, sitting among the teachers, listening to them and asking them
questions. 47 Everyone who heard him was amazed at his understanding and his answers. 48 When his
parents saw him, they were astonished. His mother said to him, "Son, why have you treated us like this?
Your father and I have been anxiously searching for you."

49 "Why were you searching for me?" he asked. "Didn't you know I had to be in my Father's house?"
50 But they did not understand what he was saying to them.

51 Then he went down to Nazareth with them and was obedient to them. But his mother treasured
all these things in her heart. 52 And Jesus grew in wisdom and stature, and in favor with God and men.

—Luke 2:41-52

Every year Joseph took his family to Jerusalem for the Passover celebrations. Up until Jesus turned twelve, we do not hear of Him causing His parents any trouble. On this particular trip however, He causes quite a stir and goes missing for three days.

If you have children, have they ever gone to a friend's house and not told you where they were going? What about your own childhood? Did you ever cause your parents fear? How did you react to your "missing" child? How did your parents react when you returned home after not telling them where you were?

How did Mary and Joseph react to Jesus' disappearance? Were they anxious? Hysterical? Angry?

Were you surprised that Mary and Joseph hadn't checked to see if all their children were present before they left for home?

The Bible does not indicate whether Joseph or Mary prayed for Jesus' safe return. We assume they did. When do you find it most difficult to trust God? How do you release your fears to Him?

“For I am the LORD, your God, who takes hold of your right hand and says to you, Do not fear; I will help you” (Isaiah 41:13).

“5 Trust in the Lord with all your heart and lean not on your own understanding;
6 in all your ways acknowledge him, and he will make your paths straight” (Proverbs 3:5-6).

What does God promise us and what is His command?

When is it easiest for you to trust God, in emergencies that require immediate action or when praying for a particular need day after day?

The book is called *Come to Me* for a reason. It isn’t just about believing in Jesus. It is about trusting Him with your life. What makes it so hard for people to let go and trust God?

Jeremiah 29:11 says, "'For I know the plans I have for you,' declares the Lord. 'Plans to prosper you and not to harm you. Plans to give you hope and a future.'"

Examine yourself. Do you really trust God with your present circumstances and your future? If it all changed tomorrow, would you still trust Him?

Prayer: Lord, Mary and Joseph trusted You in all things. When You spoke, they listened. When You told them to go, they went. Lord, the world was a scary place back then, and it is still scary. It is hard sometimes for us to let go of the little control we have. We feel safe with the familiar. It is hard for us to "let go and let God." Forgive us for not trusting You in all things. We relinquish that fear to You now. We relinquish control not only of our lives, but all those things that we still control, that we have yet to relinquish to You. Keep us mindful, Lord, when we start to take back control that we might not sin against You. May the plans You have for our lives not be thwarted by our fears. In Jesus' name. Amen.

Letting the Holy Spirit In

— Read Chapter 20 of *Come to Me* —

I don't know about you, but for many years after I found out about Jesus and believed in Him as my Saviour, I believed I needed to do things for God in order to merit His salvation. In other words, I tried very hard to be good so God would not be disappointed in me, change His mind, and revoke my salvation. Quite simply, I was terrified that, if I made a mistake, it would be the end of my relationship with the Lord.

I believed that because I did not receive proper instruction in the Word after I was saved. And so for years I kept trying to earn my salvation. I tried everything from good deeds to not swearing, drinking or doing anything that would make God angry. Unfortunately, I became so tightly wound by all my own self-imposed do's and don'ts I started to resent my relationship with this angry God who demanded so much. What I didn't see was that I was the one who was doing the demanding. I was the one imposing the rules and standards. I was the one trying to make myself good and perfect, instead of letting the Holy Spirit work within me. For many years my faith was lifeless, fake, and dull because I didn't let God do His work. And because I didn't allow Him to have full access to smooth out my rough spots, I would become incredibly nervous when talking to people about Him. Why? I didn't want to say something that was wrong about Him or offend Him. Again, my own self-imposed rules.

Today I want to look at those rough spots in our lives that need smoothing out. It is my hope that, if you are a new Christian, this lesson will help you avoid what I did early in my Christian walk. If you are further along in your faith, I believe you will still benefit from listening to what the Spirit has to say to you.

Chit-Chat: When placed in uncomfortable situations, do you clam up and keep silent or talk too much out of nervousness?

The second half of *Come to Me* follows Jesus' ministry, death, and resurrection. It begins in 68 A.D. when Luke comes to take a now very old Mary back to Ephesus to stay with John. Historical evidence can verify that John was in Ephesus in 65 A.D., after the death of Paul. He was there to reinforce the faithful and instruct them on how they should live, something Paul was concerned about, as evidenced in his letter to the Ephesians. Tradition also holds that Mary was with John in Ephesus.

It is important to note that during this time, Mary, as well as John and the other apostles, lived through the beginnings of Nero's persecutions. These persecutions came about because of the fire Nero started in Rome that almost destroyed the whole city. Nero denied starting the fire and laid the blame squarely at the feet of Christians. After that, the persecution of Christians escalated, as did the persecution of the Jews who were tired of living under the thumb of Roman rule. In 70 A.D. the Jews in Jerusalem rebelled against Rome, and as a result, the Romans destroyed Jerusalem and the Temple, as Jesus predicted before his death. (See Mark 13:2; Luke 19:41-44; Luke 21:5-6; and Luke 21:24.)

Therefore, the hatred of Jews and Christians was building when Luke went to see Mary. In light of the political climate, was Mary brave or foolish to talk about Jesus on a Roman ship?

It is one thing to share your faith with your next door neighbours who might not know the Lord, but how bold are you when sharing the gospel with total strangers? How bold are you when the situation could be risky?

How do you overcome fear?

On pages 141 and 142 of *Come to Me,* Mary mentions Isaiah 40:3-5 and insinuates that the roads the Romans built made it easier for Christians to spread the gospel. Let's look at the verse and compare it to Mary's interpretation in *Come to Me.*

"3 A voice of one calling: 'In the desert prepare the way for the Lord; make straight in the wilderness a highway for our God. 4 Every valley shall be raised up, every mountain and hill made low; the
rough ground shall become level, the rugged places a plain. 5 And the glory of the Lord will be revealed, and all mankind together will see it. For the mouth of the Lord has spoken'" (Isaiah 40:3-5).

Read verse three aloud. Does it say, "A voice of one calling in the desert..." or does it say, "A voice of one calling: In the desert..."?

What is the voice asking? Where is the voice calling for change?

Now let's look at the New Testament version of this same verse in regards to John the Baptist.

"4 A voice of one calling in the desert, 'Prepare the way for the Lord, make straight paths for him.
5 Every valley shall be filled in, every mountain and hill made low. The crooked roads shall become
straight, the rough ways smooth. 6 And all mankind will see God's salvation'" (Luke 3:4-6).

Do you think the desert is symbolic of anything?

Continuing on in verse four of Isaiah 40:3-5 and comparing it to Luke 3:4-6, how is the desert prepared?

What could the valleys, hills, and mountains represent?

"The rough ground shall become level, the rugged places a plain." What do you picture when you hear this?

What is required for people to believe in Jesus and commit their lives to Him?

Does belief in Christ come with a price for the believer? What is the cost?

Romans 5:8 says, "But God demonstrates his own love for us in this: While we were still sinners, Christ died for us."

Raising valleys and lowering mountains is no easy task. Making a straight path to the Lord is not easy either. According to Romans 5:8, does God accept us as we are in our sinful state or do we somehow have to make ourselves perfect in order to come before Him?

Spiritually speaking then, when do the rough grounds become level and the rugged places a plain?

Are you letting Jesus do His work in you or are you rebelling? How surrendered is your life to Christ?

Prayer: Lord, we confess it is not easy to live a surrendered life. Unless we begin and end our day with You, we will go about our lives never acknowledging Your presence. Forgive us. We also confess we might take You for granted. Forgive us for that too. May we keep You uppermost in our thoughts and begin each day bathed in Your Word and in prayer. Keep us from stumbling. In Jesus' name. Amen.

Working in Union with God

— Read chapters 21 and 22 of *Come to Me* —

Surrendering to God is not an easy thing to do. Most of us may think we are surrendered, when in fact we are not. It is so easy to go about your business and make decisions throughout the day without seeking God's advice or opinion at all. All too soon we end up taking back control of those things we thought we'd laid down.

Today I want to look at Mary and how she handled letting go of her son to let Him become the man He was called to be. We will also look at Jesus and how His faithful reliance on the Father kept Him in tune with the Spirit and what God was saying to Him.

Chit-Chat: As a parent, what is the hardest thing for you to let your kids do? If you do not have children, what was the most annoying thing your parents did when you were growing up?

"She would always be His mother, but at some point He must become her teacher, her Master – her Messiah." (pg. 147)

Like all mothers, Mary had a hard time letting go of her son when it was time for Him to leave home. In what ways do you relate to Mary?

How did you feel as Jesus prepared His mother for His departure?

The Greek word for master is "didaskalos." It means "one who teaches concerning the things of God, and the duties of man." The Jews would often address their teachers as Rabbi, a title used as a sign of honour even when not addressing them. In essence then, master and rabbi both mean teacher.

What is the best way to learn from Rabbi Jesus?

"Messiah" in Hebrew translates as "mashiyach." It means "anointed one." Mary knew that Jesus was God's Son and that He was destined to do great things. Even Jesus' name means "Jehovah is Salvation." Put yourself in Mary's shoes. Your child is suddenly your master (a.k.a. teacher). That's like being a modern day priest or pastor in the church. That's not too hard to accept. Many children go into the ministry. But how many require you trust completely in them for your salvation? Do you think this would have been a hard leap for Mary to make? Why or why not?

Why is it so hard for mothers to let go of their children and let them grow up?

Do you think it is easy for God to let us go and do as we please?

"11 I baptize you with water for repentance. But after me will come one who is more powerful than
I, whose sandals I am not fit to carry. He will baptize you with the Holy Spirit and with fire. 12 His
winnowing fork is in his hand, and he will clear his threshing floor, gathering his wheat into the barn
and burning up the chaff with unquenchable fire" (Matthew 3:11-12).

What was the purpose of John's baptism?

A winnowing fork separates the wheat from the chaff. The wheat is kept, and the chaff discarded. According to John, what was Jesus coming to do? Who is the wheat in this analogy, and who is the chaff?

13 Then Jesus came from Galilee to the Jordan to be baptized by John. 14 But John tried to deter him, saying, "I need to be baptized by you, and do you come to me?"

15 Jesus replied, "Let it be so now; it is proper for us to do this to fulfill all righteousness." Then John
consented.

16 As soon as Jesus was baptized, he went up out of the water. At that moment heaven was opened,
and he saw the Spirit of God descending like a dove and lighting on him. 17 And a voice from heaven said,
"This is my Son, whom I love; with him I am well pleased."

—Matthew 3:13-17

Why was it necessary for Jesus to be baptized?

29 The next day John saw Jesus coming toward him and said, "Look, the Lamb of God, who takes away
the sin of the world! 30 This is the one I meant when I said, 'A man who comes after me has surpassed me
because he was before me.' 31 I myself did not know him, but the reason I came baptizing with water was
that he might be revealed to Israel."

32 Then John gave this testimony: "I saw the Spirit come down from heaven as a dove and remain on
him. 33 I would not have known him, except that the one who sent me to baptize with water told me, 'The
man on whom you see the Spirit come down and remain is he who will baptize with the Holy Spirit.' 34 I
have seen and I testify that this is the Son of God."

—John 1:29-34

With what does Jesus baptize us?

Does baptism save you? Will it save babies?

Jesus was baptized because He had to fulfill the legal requirements for entering into the priesthood. He was a priest after the order of Melchizedek (Psalm 110:4; Hebrews 5:8-10; 6:20). Priests offered sacrifices to God on behalf of the people. To be consecrated as a priest, He had to be:

- Washed with water (Leviticus 8:6; Exodus 29:4; Matthew 3:16)
- Anointed with oil (Leviticus 8:12; Exodus 29:7; Matthew 3:16)

While Jesus was never anointed with oil at His baptism, His priesthood was affirmed by God when the Holy Spirit descended on Him like a dove. He was later anointed with oil by Mary in Bethany to prepare for His burial (John 12:1-8).

First Peter 2:9-10 says, "But you are a chosen people, a royal priesthood, a holy nation, a people belonging to God, that you may declare the praises of him who called you out of darkness into his wonderful light. Once you were not a people, but now you are the people of God; once you had not received mercy, but now you have received mercy."

After reading the verses above, do you think it is important for believers to be baptized? Why or why not?

Prayer: Lord, being a parent is hard. Teaching children to obey is difficult. We suspect You know that. Thank You for showing us, through our own children, how much You love us and how far You are willing to go to save us. Thank You also, Lord, for being obedient to the Father and for giving us an example to follow in baptism. We know, Lord, that baptism doesn't take our sins away. Only You do that. But it does symbolize repentance and the washing away of our sins. Thank You for that reminder. In Jesus' name. Amen.

Are You Wandering in the Wilderness?

—Read Chapter 23 of *Come to Me*—

We call them "desert" or "wilderness" experiences, and they are normal for most Christians. They start innocently enough – through illness, death, job loss, even the hormonal changes that come after a child's birth can bring it on through postpartum depression. And somewhere along the way, we lose our feeling of closeness to God. We become disinterested in anything to do with the church or the Bible. We make excuses to avoid our Christian friends because we don't feel "spiritual" enough. Before we know it, we are out wandering in the desert, wondering if we have lost our faith in God forever or if we were ever saved in the first place. But, by looking at Jesus' desert experience, we can have victory over Satan's attempts to lead us away from God. Today, if you are going through one of those times, it is my hope that you will be encouraged by what you find.

Chit-Chat: Have you ever had a time when you felt far away from God or began to feel disinterested in everything "spiritual"?

The Temptations of Christ

1 Then Jesus was led by the Spirit into the desert to be tempted by the devil. 2 After fasting forty days and
forty nights, he was hungry. 3 The tempter came to him and said, “If you are the Son of God, tell these
stones to become bread.”

4 Jesus answered, “It is written: ‘Man does not live on bread alone, but on every word that comes
from the mouth of God.’”

5 Then the devil took him to the holy city and had him stand on the highest point of the temple. 6
“If you are the Son of God,” he said, “throw yourself down. For it is written: ‘He will command his angels
concerning you, and they will lift you up in their hands, so that you will not strike your foot against a
stone.’”

7 Jesus answered him, “It is also written: ‘Do not put the Lord your God to the test.’”

8 Again, the devil took him to a very high mountain and showed him all the kingdoms of the world
and their splendor. 9 “All this I will give you,” he said, “If you will bow down and worship me.”

10 Jesus said to him, “Away from me, Satan! For it is written: ‘Worship the Lord your God, and serve
him only.’”

11 Then the devil left him, and angels came and attended him.

—Matthew 4:1-11

Read Matthew 4:1 again. Who led Jesus into the desert and why?

What was Jesus’ first temptation?

What was His response to Satan?

What was His second temptation?

What was His response?

What was Jesus third and final temptation?

What was His response?

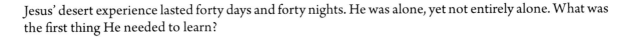

Jesus' desert experience lasted forty days and forty nights. He was alone, yet not entirely alone. What was the first thing He needed to learn?

What does this teach us? Are we ever alone during those times when God seems far away?

Jesus promised, "I will never leave you nor forsake you" (Hebrews 13:5).

We know we can trust the Lord and His promises. Yet we often feel alone and that God has left us in the lurch. More often than not, we are the ones who have strayed from God. During these times, we must remember how Satan tried to deceive Jesus when He was in the wilderness. All His temptations began with one word: if. Each temptation was meant to plant a seed of doubt in the Saviour's head. In addition, each attack was aimed at something new. We must remember Satan is always scheming to try and get us to stop believing in and trusting God.

"Be self-controlled and alert. Your enemy the devil prowls around like a roaring lion looking for someone to devour" (1 Peter 5:8).

Does God allow wilderness experiences to happen to us on purpose? Yes, indeed He does. But why? He allows us to go through these spiritually dry times in order to strengthen our faith in Him and test our faithfulness to Him. This was the very reason Jesus was led by the Holy Spirit into the desert – to be tempted to sin.

When we look at Christ's temptations in the wilderness, we begin to see a pattern in how Satan works. We can use this knowledge to our advantage to "fight against the devil's schemes" (Ephesians 6:11).

How Satan works to destroy your faith in God:

- He will cause you to doubt who you are in Christ.
- He will always attack when you are at your weakest.
- He will tempt you to test God.
- He will tempt you with what the world has to offer.
- His attempts to lead you away from God will be subtle and disguised in the form of something pleasant.

In Matthew 4:1-11, we learn Jesus was hungry. Immediately, Satan tempted Christ in two ways:

- He tried to cast doubt on who Jesus was by using that one little word we talked about earlier: if. "If you are the son of God ..." He was daring Jesus to prove Himself.
- He attacked Christ when Jesus was at His weakest: hungry for food.

Satan then goes on to tempt Jesus further, each time using the word if. He was constantly questioning Christ's divinity and authority. Jesus' response to Satan's attacks can teach us how to stand firm when we are going through our own wilderness experiences.

Five things we need to remember:

- Satan is a liar and loves to make us doubt God and our relationship with Him.
- It is important for us to memorize scripture, as it is the sword of the Spirit (Ephesians 6:17).
- God is always with us. His Holy Spirit will never leave us. EVER.
- We should never put God to the test, but trust Him no matter what happens during our wilderness experience.
- We should not try to fill the emptiness we experience during these times with things the world has to offer.

Six things that will help you survive a wilderness experience are:

- Being in the Word Daily – Read and study no matter how you are feeling.
- Trusting God in All Things – He could be testing you (Job 1:6-22).
- Praise and Worship – Praise God, especially when you don't feel like it.
- Prayer – Even feeble attempts at prayer are better than no attempts at all.
- Being in Community – Continue to go to church and meet with other Christians.
- Friends and Family – Tell someone how you are feeling, and enlist their prayers.

When is it hardest for you to trust God completely, to not try to fix things yourself?

What happens when we don't meet with God regularly and study His Word?

Wedding in Cana

1 On the third day a wedding took place at Cana in Galilee. Jesus' mother was there, 2 and Jesus and his
disciples had also been invited to the wedding. 3 When the wine was gone, Jesus' mother said to him,
"They have no more wine."

4 "Dear woman, why do you involve me?" Jesus replied. "My time has not yet come."

5 His mother said to the servants, "Do whatever he tells you."

6 Nearby stood six stone water jars, the kind used by the Jews for ceremonial washing, each holding
from twenty to thirty gallons.

7 Jesus said to the servants, "Fill the jars with water"; so they filled them to the brim.

8 Then he told them, "Now draw some out and take it to the master of the banquet." They did so, 9
and the master of the banquet tasted the water that had been turned into wine. He did not realize where
it had come from, though the servants who had drawn the water knew. Then he called the bridegroom
aside 10 and said, "Everyone brings out the choice wine first and then the cheaper wine after the guests
have had too much to drink; but you have saved the best till now."

11 This, the first of his miraculous signs, Jesus performed at Cana in Galilee. He thus revealed his
glory, and his disciples put their faith in him.

—John 2:1-11

At the wedding in Cana, Mary puts Jesus on the spot, asking Him to perform His first miracle: turning water into wine. Some things to note here are:

- Mary knew Jesus had power.
- She knew He was God's Son.
- Jesus knew He had power.
- He knew He was one with the Father.
- He felt it wasn't the appropriate time or place to use His power.
- His mother disagreed.
- He was obedient to His mother.

Was Jesus reluctant in His faith or reluctant to display His power?

If you do not spend time in prayer and Bible study daily, you can easily be deceived by Satan. You might rehash your past and be filled with regret, distancing yourself from God's healing forgiveness. You might fall prey to false teachers and be led away from the Lord. Jesus knew the Father's will because He spent time with Him daily. His faith was strengthened because of His wilderness experience, enabling Him to meet future trials, firm in the knowledge He was not alone.

What is one thing you are going to do when you start to feel yourself drifting away from God?

Prayer: Lord, Jesus experienced trials and temptations just like us. He wandered for forty days and forty nights. Lord, sometimes it feels like we have been wandering longer than that. Life can be dreadful at times. Illness, job loss, death of loved ones, and many other things haunt our days. It is during those times when we lose the desire to go on – to pray, attend church, read our Bibles. Father, we know You will never leave us nor forsake us. Help us remember that and take the lesson we have learned today with us, so that we are prepared should we ever be led into a wilderness experience. In Jesus' name. Amen.

Standing Up For Jesus

Read chapters 24, 25, and 26 in *Come to Me*

In a previous lesson we talked about how frightening it can be to share our faith. Today we are going to look at those times in our lives when we have to stand up for what is right. If Christians are silent on those things that are dear to God, who will speak up for Him? There are many issues out there today, from abortion to gay rights to the suffering Church in third world nations. There are times when we will have to champion a cause in the name of Christ. However, it is one thing to be the "voice of Christ" in causes like abortion and the suffering church. It is quite another when that voice becomes an attack. Too often, well-meaning Christians who think they are standing up for righteousness are really only causing problems within the church of Christ. For example, they show hatred for the homosexual instead of love. They show self-righteousness instead of humility. They slam the doors of the church closed on those who need it most.

In today's chapters, we see Jesus standing up and announcing to His hometown who He is. He knew how they would react. He knew what He was risking, but He did it anyway. We see Him casting out evil spirits on the Sabbath day, in a synagogue no less. And finally, we see Him giving the most important sermon ever recorded: the Sermon on the Mount. These three chapters are full of events that not only proclaim Jesus as Lord, but also show His boldness. As we reflect on this, let us remember to take that same attitude of boldness and in love and humility, share with all who seek to know the Saviour.

Note: This lesson is rather long and is split into two sections, so don't try to finish it all in one sitting. Take some time to reflect and contemplate on what you are learning and what the Spirit is telling you.

Chit-Chat: Sometimes it is easy to turn a blind eye to injustice. It is easier not to say or do anything when you know you will be reviled by those whose opinion is opposite to yours. Have you ever been in a situation where you felt the Lord leading you to speak up or felt strongly that you should voice your opinion? Did you? If so, what happened?

Sharing Jesus in Word and Deed

Read Luke 4:14-30.

When Jesus returned to Galilee, what was different about Him?

Where did Jesus teach? Where was He every Sabbath?

What do you learn about Him from this observation?

“[18] The Spirit of the Lord is on me, because he has anointed me to preach good news to the poor. He
has sent me to proclaim freedom for the prisoners and recovery of sight for the blind, to release the
oppressed, [19] to proclaim the year of the Lord’s favour” (Luke 4:18-19).

What is the first thing Jesus announces?

Jesus was anointed to do five things. What were they?

In verse 18, is Jesus talking about people who are poor financially or poor in spirit?

Is He talking about prisoners in jail or those who are prisoners of sin?

Is He speaking about the blind or those who cannot see God at work?

Who are the oppressed He came to release?

When He speaks about proclaiming the "year of the Lord's favour," what does Jesus mean?

20 Then he rolled up the scroll, gave it back to the attendant and sat down. The eyes of everyone in the
synagogue were fastened on him, 21 and he began by saying to them, "Today this scripture is fulfilled in
your hearing."

22 All spoke well of him and were amazed at the gracious words that came from his lips. "Isn't this
Joseph's son?" they asked.

23 Jesus said to them, "Surely you will quote this proverb to me: 'Physician, heal yourself! Do here
in your hometown what we have heard that you did in Capernaum.'"

—Luke 4:20-23

What did Jesus say that pits everyone against Him?

Jesus' words sparked a riot. We see this happening a lot today in the Muslim community. Words or pictures that are offensive to them seem to spark anger not unlike the anger of the Jews in today's reading. Jesus knew what would happen, yet He spoke anyway. Why do you think it was so important for Him to let His friends and neighbours know they would not accept Him?

1 One day as Jesus was standing by the Lake of Gennesaret, with the people crowding around him and
listening to the word of God, 2 he saw at the water's edge two boats, left there by the fishermen, who were
washing their nets. 3 He got into one of the boats, the one belonging to Simon, and asked him to put out
a little from shore. Then he sat down and taught the people from the boat.

4 When he had finished speaking, he said to Simon, "Put out into deep water, and let down the nets
for a catch."

5 Simon answered, "Master, we've worked hard all night and haven't caught anything. But because
you say so, I will let down the nets."
6 When they had done so, they caught such a large number of fish that their nets began to break. 7
So they signaled their partners in the other boat to come and help them, and they came and filled both
boats so full that they began to sink.
8 When Simon Peter saw this, he fell at Jesus' knees and said, "Go away from me, Lord; I am a sinful
man!" 9 For he and all his companions were astonished at the catch of fish they had taken, 10 and so were
James and John, the sons of Zebedee, Simon's partners.
Then Jesus said to Simon, "Don't be afraid; from now on you will catch men." 11 So they pulled their
boats up on shore, left everything and followed him.

—Luke 5:1-11

It is interesting to note that the four main apostles had to be wooed, so to speak, by Jesus before they surrendered all and followed Him. Simon Peter, in particular, was someone Jesus had singled out from the beginning. In *Come to Me,* it was this interest in her husband that made Perpetua fearful.

Facts about Simon Peter:

- He was wealthy enough to have employees (Mark 1:20).
- He was the only disciple whose name was changed (John 1:42).
- Jesus performed a miracle that was an object lesson for Peter and his partners (Luke 5:1-11).
- Jesus healed Peter's mother-in-law (Luke 4:38-39).
- Jesus made Peter's house his "basecamp" (Mark 1:29).
- Jesus singled out Peter, James, and John for important moments in His life (for example, the transfiguration, praying in the Garden before His arrest, etc.).
- He denied Christ three times (John 18:15-27).

Perpetua's feelings for Jesus were changed when He healed her mother. Jesus sensed a need to convince those closest to Him of His divinity. Why do you think He did this, and why was it so important?

The Beatitudes

1 Now when he saw the crowds, he went up on a mountainside and sat down. His disciples came to him,
2 and he began to teach them, saying:
3 "Blessed are the poor in spirit, for theirs is the kingdom of heaven. 4 Blessed are those who mourn,
for they will be comforted. 5 Blessed are the meek, for they will inherit the earth. 6 Blessed are those who
hunger and thirst for righteousness, for they will be filled. 7 Blessed are the merciful, for they will be
shown mercy. 8 Blessed are the pure in heart, for they will see God. 9 Blessed are the peacemakers, for
they will be called sons of God. 10 Blessed are those who are persecuted because of righteousness, for
theirs is the kingdom of heaven."

—Matthew 5:1-10

What do the poor in spirit and those who are persecuted because of righteousness receive (vs. 1 and 10)?

What is significant about this particular group of people? (See verse 1.)

I would like us to look carefully at The Beatitudes today. You will notice from the previous question that Jesus was talking to His disciples, referring to all His followers. Scripture does not say He was speaking only to the apostles, the small, select group of handpicked men He was training for ministry. This was the beginning of Jesus' famous Sermon on the Mount. He begins by telling His disciples about the blessings they would receive if they believed in Him.

- Blessed are the poor in spirit, for theirs is the kingdom of heaven. The International Standard Version translates "poor in spirit" as "destitute in spirit." God's Word Translation says, "Those who are spiritually helpless." Those who are poor in spirit realize how unworthy they are to stand before the throne of God. They agree that their sin is ever before them and without Christ they are utterly and hopelessly lost. People who are poor in spirit, therefore, recognize their spiritual condition is nothing without the saving blood of Jesus Christ. Those who acknowledge Christ as Saviour will inherit the kingdom of Heaven.

Are you poor in spirit?

- Blessed are those who mourn, for they will be comforted. Do you mourn your separation from God because of your sin? When you accept Jesus as your Saviour, your sinful state is washed clean and God sees you as a new creation, holy and perfect in His sight (2 Corinthians 5:17). What comfort to the soul that is!

Do you regret the sins you have committed? Do you weep over your separation from God?

- Blessed are the meek, for they will inherit the earth. The meek are all who have humbled themselves before God and confessed their need of Him.

Have you humbly come before your Saviour and sought His forgiveness? Have you bowed your head to God above and confessed your need of Him?

- Blessed are those who hunger and thirst for righteousness, for they will be filled. Who fills us when we seek the Lord with all our hearts? The Holy Spirit. He alone makes us complete in Christ.

Do you desire to be right with God?

- Blessed are the merciful, for they will be shown mercy. There are many opportunities to extend mercy to another. The greatest mercy of all is sharing the truth about Jesus with one who does not know Him.

God's eyes roam the earth. Will He find you merciful toward others? Have you kept the gospel to yourself or do you share it freely?

- Blessed are the pure in heart, for they will see God. "All have sinned and fall short of the glory of God" (Romans 3:23). Because of this, no one can see God face to face and live (Exodus 32:20). But those who are made new in Christ Jesus are justified by His blood and will one day see Him face to face (Revelation 22:3-4).

Have you accepted Christ as your Saviour? More importantly, have you surrendered your will to His?

- Blessed are the peacemakers, for they will be called sons of God. Are you starting to see a pattern? The Beatitudes don't single out one type of person. Jesus was describing the blessings all who follow Him will receive.

- Blessed are those who are persecuted because of righteousness, for theirs is the kingdom of heaven. Christians are currently the most persecuted people in the world. "Out of every ten people, seven cannot live their faith in full freedom. And the most persecuted faith is Christianity, with at least 200 million people suffering from discrimination."[1] Yes, serving God is a risky business, but great are the rewards for those who follow Him.

Will you risk everything to follow Jesus?

Prayer: Lord, too many times we fail to speak up when we should say something. We turn a blind eye to helping others if it is inconvenient. Help us follow Jesus' example of speaking the truth in love and showing that love through our actions. Lord, help us also remember You died for us while we were yet sinners. We don't have to change to come to You, but we do have to realize our sinful state and our need of You. Once we do that, Your Holy Spirit changes us for Your glory. Help us to submit to this transformation that we might bring glory to Your name and grow in our faith. In Jesus' name. Amen.

1 Rome Reports TV News Agency, November 30, 2010

Realizing Your Authority in Christ

— Read chapters 27 and 28 of *Come to Me* —

In today's chapters of *Come to Me,* we are going to touch on two things: our authority in Christ and the dangers we face if we do not exercise that authority. As Christians, we have a huge responsibility to those who do not know the Lord. Our lesson today may be something you've heard before, but for those of you new to the faith, it may press home exactly what you've been called to do for Jesus.

Chit-Chat: Have you ever let the opinions of others change your mind?

46 While Jesus was still talking to the crowd, his mother and brothers stood outside, wanting to speak to
him. 47 Someone told him, "Your mother and brothers are standing outside, wanting to speak to you."
48 He replied to him, "Who is my mother, and who are my brothers?" 49 Pointing to his disciples, he
said, "Here are my mother and my brothers. 50 For whoever does the will of my Father in heaven is my
brother and sister and mother."

—Matthew 12:46-50

Mary knew who her son was. Yet, in the novel, she begins to fear that Jesus' ministry would bring Him harm. She listens to her sons and agrees to bring Him home. It is then that Jesus utters those strange words from Matthew: "Who is my mother, and who are my brothers … ?"

What does this verse say to you? How does Jesus view those who believe in and follow Him?

Nicodemus came to Jesus secretly at night. He tells Jesus what he believes about Him and that is this: "Rabbi, we know you are a teacher who has come from God. For no one could perform the miraculous signs you are doing if God were not with him" (John 3:1-2).

Nicodemus observed three things about Jesus:

- He recognized that Jesus was a teacher (Rabbi).
- He recognized that Jesus was from God.
- He believed Jesus was from God because of the miracles He performed.

Jesus' response is neither a denial nor an admission to Nicodemus' claims. Instead, He says, "I tell you the truth; no one can see the kingdom of God unless he is born again" (John 3:3).

What does it mean to be born again, and why do you think Nicodemus didn't understand this term?

16 For God so loved the world that he gave his one and only Son, that whoever believes in him shall not
perish but have eternal life. 17 For God did not send his Son into the world to condemn the world, but to
save the world through him. 18 Whoever believes in him is not condemned, but whoever does not believe
stands condemned already because he has not believed in the name of God's one and only Son. 19 This is
the verdict: Light has come into the world, but men loved darkness instead of light because their deeds
were evil. 20 Everyone who does evil hates the light, and will not come into the light for fear that his deeds
will be exposed. 21 But whoever lives by the truth comes into the light, so that it may be seen plainly that
what he has done has been done through God.

—John 3:16-21

Why did God send Jesus to us?

What happens to those who do not believe in Jesus?

Who is the Light that has come into the world?

Who hates the Light and why?

Who comes to the Light and why?

Jesus asked a very pointed question of His disciples in Matthew 16:15-19. Let's read these verses together.

15 "But what about you?" he asked. "Who do you say I am?"
16 Simon Peter answered, "You are the Christ, the Son of the living God."
17 Jesus replied, "Blessed are you, Simon son of Jonah, for this was not revealed to you by man, but
by my Father in heaven. 18 And I tell you that you are Peter, and on this rock I will build my church and

the gates of Hades will not overcome it. 19 I will give you the keys of the kingdom of heaven; whatever you bind on earth will be bound in heaven, and whatever you loose on earth will be loosed in heaven."

This verse has been a source of confusion for many in regards to Peter and his authority. Peter tells Jesus that he believes Him to be the Son of the living God. How does Jesus respond? He praises Peter. He lets him know that this knowledge was revealed to him by God. Then Jesus says, "And I tell you that you are Peter, and on this rock I will build my church and the gates of Hades will not overcome it." Although Peter's name in Greek means rock, Jesus was not saying that His church would be built on Peter. He was saying that the truth of what Peter had just revealed, that Jesus was the Son of the living God, is the rock upon which His church will be built. This unshakeable foundation, that Jesus is the Messiah, is what holds and binds us together.

The translation of some of the words in this verse from English to Greek gives credence to this theory.

1. "Church" in Greek is translated "Eklasea," which means "assembly." Believers in Christ are the church. Our faith is not in Peter, but in Jesus Christ.
2. "Keys" in Greek is translated "Klas." It is a metaphor to denote power and authority. If Jesus had literally given the "keys of the kingdom" to Peter, none of us would be saved, for it would be Peter's decision alone to deny or admit us entrance to heaven. Such power and authority would never be given to one man, especially one as impulsive as Peter. This power and authority, the keys of the kingdom, was given to the body of Christ, His church.
3. "Bind" in Greek is translated "dĕō." It has enormous implications for followers of Christ as it means "to forbid or prohibit." Jesus said, "Whatever you bind on earth shall be bound in heaven." Again, if this authority was given to Peter alone, the other apostles would not have been able to cast out demons or heal the sick. Their ministry would have had no power or authority from God. If we have no power or authority in Christ, then we are useless to Him.
4. "Loose" in Greek is translated "luo." It means "to release from bondage." Jesus said, "Whatever you loose on earth, will be loosed in heaven." Spiritually speaking, who needs to be released from bondage in this world? To be set free in Christ? Those still enslaved to sin.

Even the Apostle Paul agreed that Jesus was the Rock when he said in 1 Corinthians 10:1-4, "For I do not want you to be ignorant of the fact, brothers, that our forefathers were all under the cloud and that they all passed through the sea. They were all baptized into Moses in the cloud and in the sea. They all ate the same spiritual food and drank the same spiritual drink; for they drank from the *spiritual rock* that accompanied them, and *that rock was Christ*." (Emphasis mine)

Catholicism suggests only Peter had this power and authority. Catholics believe Peter was the first pope, so the power to "bind" and "loose" was passed down from him to each pope throughout history. But scripture does not indicate this at all. As followers of Christ, we have all been called to preach the gospel to the ends of the earth. If we are silent, we keep those who are "slaves to sin" in bondage. If we do not share the gospel of Jesus Christ, we have effectively shut the door of heaven in the faces of these lost souls. However, if we are diligent in speaking the truth, we will see many come to Christ. They will break free from their bonds and enter through the gates of heaven, cleansed, forgiven, and saved for all eternity. The keys to the kingdom of heaven are found in the saving grace of our Lord and Saviour Jesus Christ. You may be someone Jesus chooses to use today to speak to someone still in bondage. How will you respond?

As Christians, we have always been aware that we alone must spread the saving message of the gospel of Jesus Christ. Yet it becomes more urgent when we realize that, by not speaking up, we risk condemning someone to eternal damnation. At the same time, by speaking up, we have opened the gates of heaven to them. Think about it. The keys of the kingdom of heaven are in your hands. How will you use them? How does this knowledge make you feel?

To review, Jesus praised Simon when he acknowledged that Jesus was the Messiah. It is in this verse where he gives Simon his new name, Peter, which means rock. Upon which rock was Jesus building his church? Peter or Jesus?

Is it possible that Peter is the foundation of the church? Why or why not?

If Jesus is building His church on the firm foundation that He is the Messiah, it is easier to see why the gates of Hades will not overcome that belief.

Based on what you've learned in this study, was Jesus giving only Peter the keys of the kingdom or was He giving them to the entire church?

Who is the key to the kingdom of Heaven?

Prayer: Father God, the implications from this verse for all believers are astonishing, overwhelming, and humbling. What an enormous task you have given us! What a responsibility! Lord, to know You didn't lay the entire burden at Peter's feet, but at the feet of every believer, to see the people in this world safely home to You, makes us realize how much we need to depend on You and take every opportunity before us to share the good news of Your saving grace. Oh, Lord, make us worthy of such an honour. In Jesus' name. Amen.

Keeping Your Focus

— Read chapters 29 and 30 of *Come to Me* —

Four important events in the life of Jesus and His disciples happened in these chapters of *Come to Me*:

- John the Baptist was beheaded.
- Jesus fed the 5,000.
- Jesus walked on water.
- Lazarus was raised from the dead.

After John the Baptist was beheaded, Jesus withdrew from the crowds to be alone. He grieved deeply for His cousin. Despite His grief, however, Jesus continued to minister to the masses. His regular habit of prayer and communion with the Father sustained Him during a very difficult time. How do you get through dark times?

Read Matthew 14:1-33.

According to Matthew 14, John's beheading, the feeding of the 5,000, and Jesus' walking on the water, all happened on the same day. Let's concentrate on the last event listed. What are your impressions of Peter when you read the story of him walking on the water toward Jesus? What qualities/character traits does he have?

Why was Peter able to walk on the water? Where was his focus?

What happened when Peter took his eyes off the Lord?

What happens to us when we take our eyes off the Lord?

In one day, the disciples experienced two incredible miracles: the feeding of the 5,000 and Jesus' walking on the water. Yet, His greatest miracle, raising Lazarus from the dead, was still to come.

Do you believe miracles still occur today? Why or why not?

Why did Jesus wait to go see Lazarus?

Jesus' faith in God was absolute. Some would say it was easy for Him to have faith in God because He was God. But Scripture is clear on this, "Jesus who, being in very nature God, did not consider equality with God something to be grasped, but made himself nothing, taking the very nature of a servant, being made in human likeness. And being found in appearance as a man, he humbled himself and became obedient to death — even death on a cross!" (Philippians 2:6-8)

Jesus had to lean on God for miracles just as much as we have to lean on God. He gave up His lordship to become one of us. When He called Lazarus out of the tomb, how did He know God would act and raise Lazarus from the dead?

Jesus once said if we had faith the size of a mustard seed, we could move mountains. Do you believe that is true? Why or why not?

What is required for miracles to occur?

What prohibits your faith from growing? How can you change that?

Prayer: Lord, our faith often takes a beating, and it is when we take our focus off You that we sink. We forge ahead without first seeking Your wisdom. Help us keep our eyes focused on You so that we can stand firm. In Jesus' name. Amen.

Sacrificial Love

— Read chapters 31 and 32 of *Come to Me* —

In many church bodies, the Lenten season is observed for forty days. Promises or "sacrifices" are made by the people of various congregations to give up something for Lent. This sacrifice is meant to draw the person closer to Christ in contemplation of the great sacrifice He made for us.

When I was younger, I remember the priest at my church reminding me at confirmation that whatever I chose to give up at Lent should be something I would really miss. It had to hurt me to be without it. Why? Because then I could understand what Jesus did for me by giving up His life. Unfortunately, my attempts at sacrifice amounted to going on a diet for forty days or giving up chewing gum. Lent became, for me at least, a competition with my friends to see who could make it through the full forty days.

Sadly, I missed the entire point: to draw closer to God and to identify with Christ and the sacrifice He had made for me. Sacrifice should hurt, or it isn't a sacrifice at all. It cost Jesus everything to lay down His life for you and me. In today's chapters, we see a beautiful portrayal of a sacrifice of worship that was offered to Jesus before He died. As you read through the chapters of *Come to Me* and answer the questions below, think about your own life. Remember that you are a "living sacrifice." How will you offer your life back to God?

Chit-Chat: Are you a Mary or a Martha? If Jesus was coming to your house for dinner, what would you do to prepare?

38 As Jesus and his disciples were on their way, he came to a village where a woman named Martha
opened her home to him. 39 She had a sister called Mary, who sat at the Lord's feet listening to what
he said. 40 But Martha was distracted by all the preparations that had to be made. She came to him and
asked, "Lord, don't you care that my sister has left me to do the work by myself? Tell her to help me!"
41 "Martha, Martha," the Lord answered, "you are worried and upset about many things, 42 but only
one thing is needed. Mary has chosen what is better, and it will not be taken away from her."

—Luke 10:38-42

What was the main difference between Martha and Mary?

Where was Mary's focus?

Where was Martha's?

Why was Martha distracted?

Would you label Martha as a complainer? Did she deliberately set out to embarrass Mary into helping her?

What did Jesus notice about Martha?

2 Here a dinner was given in Jesus' honor. Martha served, while Lazarus was among those reclining at
the table with him. 3 Then Mary took about a pint of pure nard, an expensive perfume; she poured it on
Jesus' feet and wiped his feet with her hair. And the house was filled with the fragrance of the perfume.
4 But one of his disciples, Judas Iscariot, who was later to betray him, objected, 5 "Why wasn't this
perfume sold and the money given to the poor? It was worth a year's wages." 6 He did not say this because
he cared about the poor but because he was a thief; as keeper of the money bag, he used to help himself
to what was put into it.
7 "Leave her alone," Jesus replied. "[It was intended] that she should save this perfume for the day of
my burial. 8 You will always have the poor among you, but you will not always have me."

—John 12:2-8

In Matthew 26:6-13 and Mark 14:3-9, the account of Mary anointing Jesus with perfume is different from that in the Gospel of John. John says she anointed Jesus' feet. Matthew and Mark say she poured the perfume over Jesus' head. Where she poured the perfume is not important. It is the act itself that we are going to look at today.

According to Jesus, why did Mary anoint him?

With what did she wipe Jesus' feet?

Was this a sacrifice for Mary?

Individually, we can make our own sacrifices of love to the Lord. Romans 12:1 says, "Therefore, I urge you, brothers, in view of God's mercy, to offer your bodies as living sacrifices, holy and pleasing to God – this is your spiritual act of worship." We've observed the love Mary literally poured out upon the Saviour. Her sacrifice wasn't just monetarily expensive, but it was also a sacrifice of praise and love, a very public display of affection that no doubt caused many in the room to feel uncomfortable. How do you express this kind of loving sacrifice to the Saviour?

Looking at the church body, are we failing to show the world what true sacrificial love is like? What does your church do to express its love for the Saviour?

Read Matthew 21:12-17; John 2:13-22; and Mark 11:15-19.

Jesus makes His triumphal entry into Jerusalem amidst the praises of the people. They recognize He is the Messiah. What does He do next?

"Jesus entered the temple area and drove out all who were buying and selling there. He overturned the tables of the money changers and the benches of those selling doves" (Matthew 21:12).

According to this verse, whom did Jesus drive out and why?

What is Jesus' house supposed to be called? What had it become?

Who allowed it to become that way?

Has the church today become like the temple in Jesus' day? Why or why not? Examine your own church policies. Does your church sell things on Sunday morning in the lobby? How is this different than the buying and selling in the temple during Jesus' day?

Why did the chief priests and teachers of the Law want to kill Jesus?

"14 Then one of the Twelve—the one called Judas Iscariot—went to the chief priests 15 and asked, 'What are you willing to give me if I hand him over to you?' So they counted out for him thirty silver coins. 16 From then on Judas watched for an opportunity to hand him over" (Matthew 26:14-16).

"3 Then Satan entered Judas, called Iscariot, one of the Twelve. 4 And Judas went to the chief priests and the officers of the temple guard and discussed with them how he might betray Jesus. 5 They were delighted and agreed to give him money. 6 He consented, and watched for an opportunity to hand Jesus over to them when no crowd was present" (Luke 22:3-6).

Compare the verses above. Why do you think Luke said, "Then Satan entered into him?"

Compare the religious establishment of Jesus' day to today. What similarities do you see, if any?

Would Jesus be happy with how the church body is functioning today?

Is religion something Jesus was against? Why or why not?

What needs to change in the church body today to bring it back into submission to Christ as its head?

Prayer: Lord, forgive us. We have failed to bring glory to Your name as a church body. Organized religion has people turning away from You, when instead, they should be drawn to You. We have failed to be a living sacrifice, an example to the world of Christ's love and compassion. We dole out food and clothing to help those in need while, through our words or actions, condemning those living sinful lives. Help us remember we are Your ambassadors here on earth and everything we do is a reflection of Your Spirit. Turn our hearts from religion and rituals to prayer and praise, compassion and love. Teach us the meaning of true sacrificial worship, the kind that Mary showed for You, that we may be a perfect representation of You on earth. In Jesus' name. Amen.

Are You Forgiven?

—— Read chapters 33, 34, and 35 of *Come to Me* ——

In the gospel accounts, we don't hear much about the rituals associated with the Passover Seder. In the traditional Jewish Passover feast, four cups are used. The first cup is the Cup of Sanctification, and a prayer is said over this cup called the Kiddush. This prayer acknowledges the sanctity of the day. It is said at the beginning of every Sabbath or holiday meal.

The second is the Cup of Judgement or plagues, reminding God's people of the ten plagues in Egypt. The third cup is called the Cup of Redemption, acknowledging that God redeemed the Jewish people from Egypt and the angel of death. The fourth is the Cup of Completion or praise, where the psalms of praise (Hallel) are sung.

Jesus most likely changed the meaning of the third cup, the Cup of Redemption. He changed it from a past remembrance of redemption from Egypt and the provision and protection God provided to the Israelites, to a future remembrance of the redemption He was about to accomplish on the cross. By His death, He would fulfill the sacrificial aspects of the Jewish Passover and offer protection from the wrath to come.

Today we will look closely at the Passover Seder Jesus celebrated and the new covenant He created at the Last Supper.

Chit-Chat: Have you ever participated in a Passover Seder? What was your impression?

The Last Supper

Read Luke 22:7-22; Exodus 12:1-28; and 1 Corinthians 5:8.

In Luke 22:15, Jesus tells His apostles how eager He is to share the Passover with them. In verse 16, Jesus said, "For I tell you, I will not eat it again until it finds fulfillment in the kingdom of God." Based on this verse, what will Jesus not eat again? When will He partake of it again? What does this suggest to you?

The meal began with the Cup of Sanctification. Luke 22:17-18 says, "[17]After taking the cup, he gave thanks and said, 'Take this and divide it among you. [18]For I tell you I will not drink again of the fruit of the vine until the kingdom of God comes.'"

What did Jesus do with this cup? Why is this significant?

When will Jesus drink of the "fruit of the vine" again?

During the Passover meal many rituals are observed, but Luke only touched on the first cup (the Cup of Sanctification), the bread, and the third cup of wine (the Cup of Redemption).

If you have participated in a Passover Seder, you know there is a purpose for everything on the table. All the foods symbolize something, and they are eaten in a certain order.

The use of unleavened bread symbolizes the haste with which the Israelites had to flee Egypt. Also, yeast is often a symbol of corruption and sin, so its removal from the bread symbolizes the freedom from sin that God brings. The bread itself represents affliction.

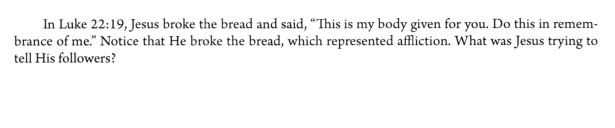

In Luke 22:19, Jesus broke the bread and said, "This is my body given for you. Do this in remembrance of me." Notice that He broke the bread, which represented affliction. What was Jesus trying to tell His followers?

Read John 13:1-17.

After dinner, Jesus showed His followers how to be servants. Why, as a Christian, is it important to have the attitude of a servant?

A foot washing during Jesus' time was standard practise. They didn't have shoes that encased the whole foot. Foot washing today, therefore, isn't something we find ourselves doing as an example of servanthood, although many Christian Seder's incorporate this act. What are some other practical ways we can serve others?

The Last Supper is called that for a reason. Jesus said He would not partake of the fruit of the vine again until the kingdom of God comes. Jesus said in Luke 22:20, "This cup is the new covenant in my blood, which is poured out for you." This command to His church has become one of the most important ordinances in all Christian churches. Communion, as it has come to be known, is celebrated every week in some churches. In others, it is observed once a month.

The Passover was a sacred Feast during Jesus' time and still is today to the Jews. It is to be celebrated once a year in remembrance of their deliverance and redemption from Egypt. In Luke 22:15-16, Jesus-said, "I have eagerly desired to eat this Passover with you before I suffer. For I tell you, I will not eat it again until it finds fulfillment in the kingdom of God."

Here are some questions to get you thinking. Keep in mind that Jesus celebrated the Passover and it was the Passover ritual that He followed. Should the church be observing Passover or communion once a year as our Lord did? Why or why not?

After they had celebrated the Passover dinner, Jesus took His disciples to Gethsemane and spent the night praying. Much was about to happen, and it would be the final temptation of Christ.

The Final Temptation

Have you ever been ridiculed for your faith? How did you react? How did you feel afterwards?

Read Matthew 26:36-75.

Whom did Jesus take with Him into the garden?

What did He ask them to do? Why?

What did Jesus ask of God?

How long did Jesus pray the first time?

What did Jesus say to Peter specifically when He came back and found them sleeping?

Why do you think He singled out Peter as opposed to everyone else?

Why did Peter deny Christ? What was the driving force behind his denial?

What was Peter's reaction when he realized he had denied the Lord?

What was Judas' reaction when he realized what he had done?

Was Peter forgiven? Why or why not?

Was Judas? Why or why not?

What is the difference between remorse and repentance?

How then do we know we are forgiven for our sins? What is the attitude we should have?

1 John 1:9 says, “If we confess our sins, He is faithful and just and will forgive us our sins and cleanse us from all unrighteousness.”

Take some time now before the Lord. Think about the sacrifice He made for you. Examine your heart and confess your sins, knowing that the Lord will forgive you and cleanse you from all unrighteousness.

Prayer: Lord, You clearly showed us who You are. The Passover Seder perfectly talks of Your sacrifice for us. You loved us so much You laid down Your life for us. We confess there have been times when we have not honoured the sacrifice You made for us. We do it by our actions or inaction. We think we would never deny You, yet we have never been in Peter’s situation. Our brothers and sisters on the other side of the world are facing persecution daily because they will not deny You. Lord, when our time comes, keep us faithful and strong. In Jesus’ name. Amen.

Why Did Jesus Die for You?

—Read chapters 36, 37, and 38 of *Come to Me*—

Unruly mobs have a way of inciting otherwise peaceful people to commit horrible acts. In 2011, after the Canucks did not bring home the Stanley Cup, riots broke out. One young man, who plays water polo on Canada's junior national team and who aspired to be in the Olympics, got caught up in the mayhem and lit a police car on fire. He made a public apology, but the damage had already been done. Our actions speak louder than words as to our character.

The actions of the Sanhedrin, particularly those of Caiaphas, tell us a great deal about the character of these priests of God who had control over the Jewish people. The amazing thing about these men was the fact that they banded together, not to try to find out if the Messiah had actually come in the form of Jesus, but to prove Jesus wasn't the Messiah. It seems odd that men who claimed to be priests of God would not carefully search the Scriptures for their answers. Instead, in a show of self-righteous indignation, they condemned Jesus to death. Was it fear of losing their lofty positions in office that drove them to such an act? I've no doubt it was this attitude that provoked them into arresting Jesus and putting Him on trial. We may wonder how the priests managed to get the Jews, who had proclaimed Jesus as Messiah the week before when He rode into Jerusalem on a donkey, to turn against Him so easily. Yet we know from the Stanley Cup riots and others we have seen on TV that it doesn't take much to get people riled up.

Chit-Chat: Is getting caught up in the moment justifiable? Have you ever bowed to peer pressure? What was the outcome?

What is Truth?

You will need your Bible today. Please read Matthew 27:11-26; Luke 23:1-25; John 18:28-19:16.

Why did Caiaphas and those in the Sanhedrin want Jesus killed?

How did Pilate initially react to Jesus?

How many times did he try to save Jesus?

How did he try to placate the Jews?

Was Pilate guilty of Jesus death? Why or why not?

What was the deciding factor in Pilate handing Jesus over to the Jews?

Jesus said in John 18:37, "… For this reason I was born, and for this I came into the world, to testify to the truth. Everyone on the side of truth listens to me."

According to this verse, why did Jesus come into the world?

"Jesus answered, 'I am the way and the truth and the life. No one comes to the Father except through me'" (John 14:6).

"Sanctify them by the truth; your word is truth" (John 17:17).

Who and what is the truth?

Do you believe this? Why or why not?

The Crucifixion

How do you deal with grief? To whom do you turn when your suffering is so great you cannot bear it anymore?

Read Matthew 27:32-61; Mark 15:21-47; Luke 23:26-56; and John 19:17-42.

Was the chapter on the crucifixion difficult for you to read in Come to Me? Why or why not?

Why did Jesus willingly give up His life for us?

28 Jesus turned and said to them, "Daughters of Jerusalem, do not weep for me; weep for yourselves and
for your children. 29 For the time will come when you will say, 'Blessed are the barren women, the wombs
that never bore and the breasts that never nursed!' 30 Then they will say to the mountains, 'Fall on us!'
and to the hills, 'Cover us!'
31 For if men do these things when the tree is green, what will happen when it is dry?"

—Luke 23:28-31

In Luke 23:28-31, Jesus spoke to the women who were mourning for Him. What did He tell them not to do?

What did Jesus mean in verse 31 when He said, "For if men do these things when the tree is green, what will happen when it is dry?" Who or what does the tree symbolize?

Two thousand years later, is the tree dry or still green?

What does Jesus' crucifixion mean to you?

Imagine you are Mary watching this horrible thing happen to your son. What would you do?

Jesus uttered the words, "It is finished." To what was He referring?

How should you live in light of what He has done for you?

If you have not acknowledged Christ as your Saviour or accepted His gift of salvation, what holds you back?

If you have received Christ as your Saviour, share your testimony with others in your group as time allows. If you are studying this on your own, make a point of going "out into the world" this week and share with someone the good news of salvation that is found in Jesus Christ our Lord.

Prayer: Lord, we have learned that Your Word is truth and that You came into the world to testify to the truth. Keep us faithful to Your Word and in it daily, so that the father of lies might not deceive us. Lord, it is upsetting for us to read in graphic detail how much You suffered for us. We are ashamed that You had to endure so much because of our sin. Lord, You brought us life and freedom from slavery to the lies of the evil one. Forgive us, Lord, if we have taken Your sacrifice and death for granted. May we go out into the world this week, renewed in our faith and commitment to You. In Jesus' name. Amen.

Jesus' Death & Resurrection

—— Read chapters 39 and 40 of *Come to Me* ——

Many are confused about the timing of Jesus' death and resurrection. Some insist that a full three days could not have passed for Him to rise on a Sunday, so today we are going to look at this in the terms of Jewish history and the Jewish calendar.

The Passover and the Feast of Unleavened Bread are two very important feasts instituted by God. Leviticus 23:4-8 says, "These are the Lord's appointed feasts, the sacred assemblies you are to proclaim at their appointed times: The Lord's Passover begins at twilight on the fourteenth day of the first month. On the fifteenth day of that month the Lord's Feast of Unleavened Bread begins; for seven days you must eat bread made without yeast. On the first day hold a sacred assembly and do no regular work. For seven days, present an offering made to the LORD by fire. And on the seventh day hold a sacred assembly and do no regular work."

The Jewish people observed their days differently. A new day began for the Jew at sunrise and did not end until sunset. A Roman day, however, went from midnight to midnight, just like ours. When we are interpreting Scripture, it is important to keep these historical facts in mind. It is also important to remember the Passover was not just one day. It was a festival that was celebrated throughout the week.

Chit-Chat: When you see a commercial on TV for a product that looks too good to be true, do you find out if someone else has used it, read testimonials, or go out and buy it because the commercial convinced you? What does it take to convince you of something that seems impossible?

Using the chart on the following pages, answer these questions:

According to Leviticus 23:4-8, when did the Passover begin?

When did the Feast of Unleavened Bread begin?

When did the disciples prepare the Passover meal? See Matthew 26:17.

According to a Jewish day then, when was the Last Supper?

Using the chart provided, when was Jesus arrested?

According to a Jewish day, when did Jesus' trial begin?

What day of the week was it for the Romans?

At what hour was Jesus crucified? See Mark 15:25.

At what time did the darkness come over the land?

At what hour did Jesus die?

What did the Chief Priests and Pharisees do on the Sabbath, a day of rest? See Matthew 27:62-66.

What day of the week did Jesus rise from the dead?

According to a Jewish day, how many days was He dead? When did He say He would rise again?

Why do you suppose, after seeing angels, Mary Magdalene still thought someone had taken Jesus?

24 Now Thomas (called Didymus), one of the Twelve, was not with the disciples when Jesus came. 25 So
the other disciples told him, "We have seen the Lord!"
But he said to them, "Unless I see the nail marks in his hands and put my finger where the nails
were, and put my hand into his side, I will not believe it."
26 A week later his disciples were in the house again and Thomas was with them. Though the doors
were locked, Jesus came and stood among them and said, "Peace be with you!" 27 Then he said to Thomas, "Put your finger here; see my hands. Reach out your hand and put it into my side. Stop doubting and
believe."
28 Thomas said to him, "My Lord and my God!"

29 Then Jesus told him, "Because you have seen me, you have believed; blessed are those who have not seen and yet have believed."

—John 20:24-29

Jesus appeared to everyone in the Upper Room the same night He rose from the dead. The only apostle missing was Thomas and he reacted with doubt. What do you think of his reaction? What would you have done?

One week later, Jesus appeared to Thomas and he finally believed. What does Jesus say in John 20:29 about those who believe without seeing Him? How does that make you feel?

The Gospels are eyewitness accounts of Jesus' death and resurrection. Are they enough to convince you Jesus is the Son of God? Why or why not?

Prayer: Lord, sometimes seeing is believing, and many people need miracles to actually believe You are real. Even after Mary told Peter You had risen, he and John still had to go to the tomb to find out for themselves. Lord, forgive us for when we doubt. Help us to know why we believe. Strengthen our faith. In Jesus' name. Amen.

Timeline of Events

Day	What Happened	Scripture References	Jewish Timeline
Thursday Morning	Passover Preparation	Matthew 26:17 Mark 14:12 Luke 22:7-8	15 Nisan
Thursday Evening	Jesus observes the Passover; washes apostles feet; Judas leaves the supper; Jesus foretells of His betrayal and Peter's denial; Jesus institutes the Lord's Supper; Jesus' final discourse	Luke 22:14-38 John 13:1-14:31 Matthew 26:20-35	15 Nisan
Thursday Late	Jesus walks to Gethsemane, prays, is betrayed, arrested, and all His disciples flee.	Matthew 26:36-56 Luke 22:39-53 Mark 14:32-51 John 18:1-11	15 Nisan Jesus' trial was held while all of Jerusalem slept.
Friday Morning (pre-dawn)	First stage of Jewish trial, Jesus before Annas; Peter's first denial.	John 18:12-27	15 Nisan Technically still Thursday until the sun rises
Friday Morning (early dawn)	Second stage of Jewish trial, Jesus before Caiaphas and Sanhedrin.	John. 18:24 Matthew. 26:57-68	15 Nisan

Friday Morning (late dawn)	Third stage of Jewish trial, Jesus formerly condemned by the Sanhedrin and led to Pilate; Peter denies Christ two more times.	Luke 22:58-23:1	15 Nisan A Jewish day begins when the sun rises.
Friday Morning (sunrise begins)	First stage of Roman trial, Jesus before Pilate.	John 18:28-38	15 Nisan Friday is about to begin in the Jewish Calendar.
Friday Morning (sunrise continues)	Second stage of Roman trial, Jesus before Herod.	Luke 23:6-12	15 Nisan
Friday Sunrise	Third stage of Roman trial, Pilate has Jesus scourged and sentences Him to death.	John 18:39-19:16 Matthew 27:15-30	16 Nisan Friday officially begins at 6:00 am.
Friday Morning	Judas remorseful and hangs himself.	Matthew 27:3-10	16 Nisan This is also known as Preparation Day (the day before the Sabbath).
Friday morning 8:00-8:30 am	Jesus led out to be crucified.	Matthew 27:31-34	16 Nisan
Friday Morning 9:00 am	Jesus is crucified.	Matthew 27:35-56 Mark 15:24-41 Luke 23:33-49 John 19:17-37	16 Nisan Third hour of the day
Friday Afternoon 12:00 pm	Darkness comes upon the land.	Mark 15:33	16 Nisan Sixth hour of the day
Friday Afternoon 3:00 pm	Jesus dies; the temple curtain is torn in two.	Matthew 27:35-56 Mark 15:24-41 Luke 23:33-49 John 19:17-37	16 Nisan Ninth Hour (1st day)
Friday Evening	Jesus is buried.	Matthew 27:57-61 Mark 15:42-47 Luke 23:50-56 John 19:38-42	16 Nisan Sunset is close, and the Sabbath is about to begin.

Friday Sunset	Jesus is in the tomb.		17 Nisan The Sabbath has begun. (2nd day)
Saturday	Chief Priests and Pharisees go to Pilate and ask for Jesus' tomb to be secured by a guard.	Matthew 27:62-66	17 Nisan A day to rest (2nd day)
Sunday Sunrise	The women go to the tomb, discover Jesus has risen, and alert disciples.	Matthew 28:1-10 Mark 16:1-7 Luke 24:1-12 John 20:1-18	18 Nisan (3rd day)
Sunday Afternoon	Jesus appears on the road to Emmaus	Luke 24:13-35	18 Nisan Before the Sabbath begins
Sunday Evening	Jesus appears to his disciples.	John 20:19	19 Nisan (4th day)

Are You Ready?

— Read chapter 41 and Epilogue of *Come to Me* —

Forgiveness is probably one of the hardest things to offer someone who has done us wrong. I know of a woman whose brother was murdered and she found it in her heart to forgive the murderer. Today that woman, Annette Stanwick, author of *Forgiveness: The Mystery and Miracle*, along with her husband, minister to men like her brother's murderer in our prison system. How does she do it? How does anyone find the grace to forgive when they've been horribly hurt by another? It can only be done through the work of the Holy Spirit and a person's willingness to surrender to the Lord's will.

But there is another type of forgiveness that many people struggle with. It is not born from the hurt of another. It is the inability to forgive ourselves. Like Peter, we may be plagued with guilt for past mistakes. If we have been the one to harm another, we seem to be able to ask the person for forgiveness. Yet, when it is given, we don't take it to heart. We hold onto the guilt as a form of punishment, and we inevitably sink into the pits of despair and depression.

Today we will look at how the Lord helped Peter climb out of that pit of despair. It is my hope that, if you are still holding onto regrets for your past mistakes, you will learn, like Peter did, that Jesus loves you and forgives you as well.

Chit-Chat: What is harder for you to do, forgive someone or forgive yourself?

Read John 21:1-25.

Why do you suppose Jesus asked Peter three times if he loved Him?

How did that make you feel, knowing that Jesus cared enough to help Peter forgive himself?

"30 He who is not with me is against me, and he who does not gather with me scatters. 31 And so I tell you, every sin and blasphemy will be forgiven men, but blasphemy against the Spirit will not be forgiven. 32 Anyone who speaks a word against the Son of Man will be forgiven, but anyone who speaks against the Holy Spirit will not be forgiven, either in this age or in the age to come" (Matthew 12:30-32).

According to Webster's dictionary, blasphemy is "the act of insulting or showing contempt or lack of reverence for God."

In Matthew 12:30-32, what sins does God forgive?

Does He forgive the sin of blasphemy against Himself?

John 3:16 says, "For God so loved the world He gave His only begotten Son, so that whoever believes in Him shall not perish, but have eternal life."

John 3:36 says, "Whoever believes in the Son has eternal life, but whoever rejects the Son will not see life, for God's wrath remains on him."

The Holy Spirit is God's divine presence that dwells within His followers. Blasphemy against the Holy Spirit is, in essence, rejecting God. Therefore, anyone who does not believe in the Son and rejects His gift of eternal life is committing blasphemy against the Holy Spirit.

Does God ever forgive blasphemy against the Holy Spirit?

Knowing this, is there any sin you have committed that God will not forgive?

Read John 21:15-23.

Why do you think Jesus told Peter how he was going to die?

When Jesus asked Peter to follow Him, Peter turned back, saw the Apostle John, and asked, "Lord, what about him?" What was Jesus' response to Peter?

Was Peter comparing himself to John? What can we learn from this?

Knowing about Jesus is not enough to save you. Going to church every Sunday will not save you. Doing good deeds will not save you either. There is only one way we can be saved, and we have learned from our study that Jesus is the only way.

As Luke stated in *Come to Me*, "No one deserves the gift of salvation Jesus offers us, but in His loving mercy, our Father wants us to take it, to come back into fellowship with Him."

Surrendering ourselves completely to God leaves us vulnerable. It scares us because we do not know what God will ask us to do. However, it is a necessary step if we are to live in communion with God.

Surrendering to Christ is a daily, intentional way of living. Are you a Christian in name only, or are you walking in step with the Father, Son, and Holy Spirit?

If you have not experienced life with Christ, what holds you back?

Jesus said, "I tell you, whoever acknowledges me before men, the Son of Man will also acknowledge him before the angels of God" (Luke 12:8).

He is returning soon. Will He acknowledge you before His Father?

Prayer: Lord, it won't be easy living our lives unselfishly. Before we acknowledged You as Saviour, we could get up and go about our day without a care in the world. Now there is something bigger than we are in our lives, and we want to honour that. May our lives be a reflection of Your glory. May the words we speak be an encouragement to others. May our hands minister to those You send our way. In everything we do, may it all be directed by You. We surrender all to You, Lord. We are Your faithful servants. Amen.

CPSIA information can be obtained at www.ICGtesting.com
Printed in the USA
LVOW112313050412

276383LV00003B/4/P

9 781770 695122